Welcome to the 10th edition of Itchy. Whet[...]
you're an Itchy virgin or an old flame, we'[...]
here to help you make the most of going [...]
in Bath. We hope you enjoy yourselves as
much as we have over the last 10 years...

GW01071946

IN-HOUSE TEAM

Editor: Mike Toller

Local editor: Joly Braime

Features editor: Alexi Duggins

Editorial and production assistants:
Clare Cullen, Alix Fox

Editorial assistants: Jon Lynes, Anton Tweedale

Editorial assistance: Iliana Dracou, Sam Shields,
Achmed Esser, Cory Burdette, Lily Gorlin,
Rozanne Gelbinovich, Maisie McCabe,
Julie Dyer, Jackie Fishman

Designers: Paul Jones, Sara Gramner

Design assistance: Katelyn Boller

Picture research: Tiago Genoveze,
Philip Kelly, Neha Bhargava, Katelyn Boller

Production consultant: Iain Leslie

National ad sales: Sue Ostler, Zee Ahmad

Local ad sales: Catherine Farinha

Distribution: Efua Hagan

Financial controller: Sharon Watkins

Managing director: Ian Merricks

Publisher: Itchy Group

© 2008 Itchy Group

ISBN: 978-1-905705-28-3

City editor: Daniel Coleman

Contributors: Amy Gardner, Claire Sartin,
Hamish Chant-Sempill, Corinne Randall,
Stewart Foster, Dame Amy

Photography: Anna White, Tim Ireland, Juliet
Hookey, Nicky Tiney, James Kergozou, SXC,
Tiago Genoveze, Roland Eva, Chris Grossmeier

Cover and feature illustrations: www.si-clark.co.uk

Itchy

Itchy Group
78 Liverpool Road, London, N1 0QD
Tel: 020 7288 9810
Fax: 020 7288 9815
E-mail: editor@itchymedia.co.uk
Web: www.itchycity.co.uk

Itchy
Contents

Introduction

Welcome to Bath, welcome to Itchy. Here's the lowdown on all the high life

Eat

Hungry? We know where you can fill your boots and bellies

Dance

From hot-steppers to headbangers, we've got good news for anyone who wants to shake it

Drink

There's nothing like going for a drink or 12. Wet your whistles in these pubs and bars

Contents

ITCHY-10TH-BIRTHDAY-ITCHY-10TH-

81

BACKSTAGE

Welcome to Bath

THEY CAME, THEY SAW, THEY CONQUERED

Happy birthday to us, happy birthday to us, happy birthday dear u-us, happy birthday to us. We can hardly believe it's been 10 years since we first opened our pages to the sights and sounds of beautiful Bath. But don't worry, we're not quite ready for the knacker's yard just yet (and when we do get sent down, we're taking you with us). We're still brimming with excitement at all things Bath. Unlike some children, we were always excited by the prospect of Bath-time, so combine that with Romans and you're laughing. With a pinch of Jane Austen thrown in for good measure, you get one of the most elegantly laid out cities to graces this septic isle. And it's not all books and history, if you're worried. This town knows how to party. Small but perfectly formed, this is a Bath you don't need a rubber ducky to enjoy. So, let's all hold hands and take a deep breath as we plunge headlong into the brilliance and the beauty of Bath.

10 years

Changes in Bath over the last ten years

IT'S BEEN 10 YEARS SINCE ITCHY FIRST SET FOOT IN BATH. AND YOU'LL BE HAPPY TO KNOW THAT IN SOME CASES NOT MUCH HAS CHANGED. COME ON, NO ONE VISITS BATH FOR IT'S CUTTING-EDGE MODERNIST ARCHITECTURE, SO WE GUESS YOU'LL BE HAPPY TO KNOW THAT THE GEORGIAN SPLENDOUR IS STILL INTACT. WHEN THAT MEANS YOU CAN STILL ENJOY LOCAL CIDER IN A 16TH CENTURY PUB, FOLLOWED BY A STROLL AROUND THE CHOCOLATE-BOX SURROUNDINGS – WHAT'S NOT TO LIKE?

Well… the city does have a reputation for being a touch reactionary. For example, the council's recent decision to turn down James Dyson's proposed multimillion-pound design centre in Bath. Cue hoards of liberal newspaper critics denouncing Bath as backward and wilfully old-fashioned. However, there is one aspect of life at least in which Bath has kept pace with the rest of the nation – drinking. Depending on your tastes, Bath is a regrettable regular on *Booze Britain*, complete with footage of mini-skirted and Ben Sherman-ed adolescents yelling at the camera. However, if you give the WKD a wide berth then extended licensing laws can definitely be used to your advantage…

Rather than feeling claustrophobic, most enjoy how tiny Bath is. It's great to be able to get to know the city in a long weekend, even better to bump into our friends in the street. A bit like *Cheers* – only across a whole town. Its compact size only increases the satisfaction in discovering a gem of a café squirrelled away in some unknown corner.

Itchy also loves the new additions to Bath's music scene. Moles has really stepped up Bath's profile by bringing regular big-name bands to its music night, Pulp. Rather than being a musical black hole between London and Cardiff, Bath is becoming a must-play destination on the band circuit. Finally, it's important to remember that Bath is a University town and contrary to the reports of *Booze Britain*, students are good for more than decorating the cobbles with their sick. Both Bath and Bath Spa Uni host great ents nights, both off and on campus. In fact, the newly revamped ICIA arts centre at the Bath campus is a great place to get your hit of avant-garde theatre and music. We like cute little Bath, and yes, we reckon that great things really do come in small packages.

Introduction

Local Lingo

IF YOU WANT TO BLEND IN WITH THE CIDER-SWILLING LOCALS THEN IT'LL HELP TO BE FAMILIAR WITH BATH'S 'DISTINCTIVE' LINGO. FIRSTLY – YES, IT'S REALLY TRUE – ADOPTING A FARMER'S ACCENT IS CRUCIAL IN SOUNDING AUTHENTIC. TO EXPRESS APPROVAL FOR THE HOT CHICK AT THE BAR/YOUR PINT, USE EITHER 'MINT, INNIT?' OR 'GERT LUSH'. IF THAT 'MACKY BUZZER' SKULKING MENACINGLY IN THE CORNER KICKS OFF, TURN TO YOUR NEIGHBOUR AND SAY 'EE'S ROIGHT BAITEY, THREW A PROPER BENNY' (HE'S IN A BAD MOOD, REALLY LOST HIS TEMPER). FINALLY, TRY TO COMPLICATE YOUR SPEECH BY ADDING UNNECESSARY WORDS: 'WHERE'S THAT TO?' INSTEAD OF 'WHERE'S THAT'. YOU GET THE PICTURE. AND DON'T FORGET TO DROP YOUR 'ING'S – THE SNOW IS 'PITCHIN' TONIGHT, FOLKS…

Top five places to have your photo taken

Bath's historical roots make for great photo opportunities. Don a bonnet and bustle and parade up and down the Royal Crescent, Jane Austen style.

Look like you've been to Iceland for a mini-break without actually having to splash out on £10 pints by posing with some blondes in the Thermae Spa. Be careful taking 'holiday snaps' though, unless you're desperate to get kicked out onto the street in only your Speedos.

Leave your 'photographic evidence' of supernatural entities for the Ghost Walk, it's much better suited to strange sightings (for guaranteed results we suggest a strategically placed finger on the camera lens...)

Don the garb of a Roman Centurion and set up shop outside the Roman Baths. You will almost certainly be able to persuade tourists that they should pay you upwards of a fiver for the privilege of having their photo taken with a real Roman.

And best of all, try to fake a safari by getting snapped with the monkeys at Longleat – but beware, they bite.

Quirky facts

'Ooh, go on – intrigue me', we hear you say. 'Tell me something I've never heard before and won't hear anywhere else'. Well, did you know that the world's first postmark was stamped 'Bath' on May 2nd 1840? – No, we didn't think you would. Where was it going to? Peckham, naturally.

Perhaps Bath's most unlikely resident is Hollywood superstar, Nicolas Cage. Although it's somewhat less surprising to hear that he lives in a £4 million town house which was once the home of the Earl of Chatham.

Bath's most famous ghost is simply referred to as 'the man in the black hat'. He's dressed in a top hat and billowing black cloak – apparently the best places to look for him are the near the Assembly Rooms and on Saville Row.

Although easily the city's most famous resident, Jane Austen more or less hated Bath and was greatly relieved when her family moved. This hasn't stopped the city from cashing in BIG TIME on the Austen industry. So thank you, Jane, and thank you, the BBC for keeping us afloat.

Eat

Eat

Welcome to Eat

Slacken your belt another notch, as Bath is bursting with gastronomic delights. Kill a hangover the scenic way by enjoying a breakfast by the water at **The Riverside Café (17 Argyle Street, 01225 480 532)**. For a right royal roast, indulge at the **Hole in the Wall (16 George Street, 01225 425 242)**. It doesn't come cheap, but then it does have the reputation of being Bath's best restaurant. Vegetarians are in for a treat at Demuths Vegetarian **(2 North Parade Passage, 01225 446 059)**. It's daring cuisine that doesn't try to replace meat with stuffed peppers.

Top five cheap eats

Bottelinos – great veggie options and cheap pizzas.

Wagamama – these restaurants are everywhere for a reason: it's fast, it's cheap, it's tasty and they irreverently write on your place mat.

Eastern Eye – impeccable curry, service and surroundings at reasonable prices.

F.east – 60 dishes at £6.50 each. Bargain.

Yum Yum Thai – good value food that isn't OTT.

Top five places for a posh meal

Le Beaujolais – fine dining at its best. Steak tartare, anyone?

Le Flamma – it's got to be a good sign when the wine comes from their own vineyard.

Rajpoot – for those who like to eat their curry with a silver spoon.

Fishworks – sophisticated food and not an upturned nose in sight.

The Pump Rooms – perfect for afternoon tea, complete with dainty plates and cucumber sandwiches.

How to get your meal for *Free*

'THE BEST THINGS IN LIFE ARE FREE', SANG JANET JACKSON AND LUTHER VANDROSS. AND WHO ARE WE TO ARGUE WITH SOMEONE WHO HAS THE WORD 'DROSS' IN THEIR SURNAME? HERE, THEN, ARE ITCHY'S TIPS FOR GETTING YOUR MEAL FOR FREE WHEN DINING OUT

Take offence – What do they mean they're a steak restaurant? You're a vegetarian, goddammit, and the very presence of a piece of meat on your plate constitutes a grave slur against your lifestyle. Though a free meal might stop you calling your animal rights activist mates.

Spot a 'rodent' – Bag yourself some form of wind-up animal toy, and unleash it across the floor of your restaurant. As soon as you release, leap up screaming, 'Mouse! Mouse!' in the most hysterical voice you can manage. Have an accomplice waiting to retrieve the toy in the confusion, and they'll have to let you off paying to make it up to you.

Make up a stupid food allergy Food allergies are all the rage nowadays; you can get away with pretending you're allergic to pretty much anything. Make up an allergy to something suitably ludicrous, then nip to the toilets, inflate a balloon, stuff it down the neck of your top, and draw on your face with red felt tip. Hey presto: instant swollen throat and rash. They're bound to give you a freebie after doing all that to poor old you.

Fake narcolepsy – Every time the waiter attempts to present you with the bill, pretend to drop off. No way can they charge you if they can't rouse you. Sooner or later they'll give up and carry you out onto the street, where you can sneak away with a belly as full as your wallet.

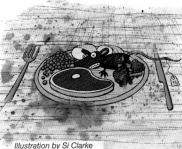

Illustration by Si Clarke

Eat

CAFÉS

Adventure Café and Bar

5 Princes Buildings, George Street

(01225) 462 038

We'd go here even if all it served was sachets of ketchup, small salt packets and sparkling mineral water sourced from Botswana. There's something about the atmosphere that's so satisfying you just want one of the pretty girls at the bar to cradle you and stroke your hair until you drift off pleasantly into dreams about spending every waking second of your life here, drinking lattes and snacking on lunches in a daze of euphoria. Or maybe that's just us.

🕐 Sun–Tue, 10am–5pm;
Wed–Sat, 10am–11pm
🍴 Selection of sandwiches, £4.95

Blackstone's Kitchens

10a Queen Street

(01225) 338 803

Blackstone's has cleverly cornered the market for lunch in Bath. What they did was actually just to create really good food and then sell it. It's as simple as that, although don't let the 'gourmet takeaway' get you thinking you'll be tucking into foie gras and beluga. It's much more wholesome and hearty than all that. Visit Blackstone's and you'll get a weekly changing menu of soups, stews and sandwiches with a restaurant twist to them. The queues are so big, some have been known to set up camp outside the night before. Well, not really. But it is popular.

🕐 Mon–Fri, 7.30am–4pm; Sat, 8.30am–4pm
🍴 Roast in a roll, £3.75

Bongy Bo's

2–3 Barton Court,

(01225) 462 276

When is a Chinese not a Chinese? When it's an Italian, or when it's a cake shop. Bongy Bo's isn't fusion food, and it's definitely not the enigma of 'Pan-Asian', but as noodles, lasagne and carrot cake battle for your taste buds, confusion reigns. It's a bamboo restaurant without bamboo. It's like eating ice cream while smelling curry. It's like eating tagliatelle while being surrounded by onion bhajis. But yet, strangely enough, despite this apparent crisis of identity, it all comes together in the end, like oddly-paired lovers.

🕐 Mon–Sat, 9am–7pm; Sun, 9am–6pm
🍴 Sandwiches, £2–3
🍷 Glass house wine, £3.15

Boston Tea Party

19 Kingsmead Square

(01225) 313 901

A popular place to sit and enjoy a proper coffee the morning after the night before and a perfect place for people watching. Situated on busy Kingsmead Square, you can sit al fresco near an ancient tree, which attracts tourist photographers alongside the local winos. We find there's nothing quite like listening to a tramp serenading you while you sit down for a bit of breakfast. All the food is organic and locally produced, which means it's tasty and ethical – perfect for those days when you need to feel good about yourself.

🕒 *Mon–Sat, 7.30am–7pm;*
Sun, 9am–7pm

🍴 *Falafel wrap, £5.95*

Café Shoon

14 Old Bond Street

(01225) 480 095

Above a shop that sells top label clothes at top prices is a little café that reeks of inexpensive bohemia. Shoon is brilliant for veggies and vegans alike, so it stops the 'where shall we eat?' row. Unpretentious food, soups thick enough to clog a straw, and quiche and sandwiches to stretch your jaw. Great local juices and fresh smoothies. We were served by a Jeff Goldblum lookalike; lovely bloke, shame he blows his nose so much, but this place is too good to wait for the hayfever season to end.

🕒 *Café, Mon–Sat, 9.30am–5pm; Sun,*
11am–4pm; shop, Mon–Sat, 9.30am–6pm;
Sun, 11am–5pm

🍴 *Sandwiches and melts, from £4.95*

Café Retro

18 York Street

(01225) 339 347

Save yourself a wasted trip to the Moulin Rouge and visit this little ticket office of a café. It's sexier than a pouting Catherine Deneuve in black silk/Itchy perched seductively on a bed in a sequined thong. Having said that, it's not so much retro as an old wooden bar that looks like a Punch and Judy show will be starting there every half hour. They serve up really tasty food at prices just high enough to keep the over 60s from sitting there and nursing a cup of tea form three hours, but cheap enough to sit and cuddle your teddy bear.

🕒 *Mon–Sat, 9am–6pm; Sun, 10am–6pm;*
Thu–Sat, 6.30pm–11pm

🍴 *Retro Skyscraper, £5.80*

Eat

The Fine Cheese Co Café

29–31 Walcot Street

(01225) 483 407

Wandering around The Fine Cheese Co. – home to some of the tastiest cheeses any deli in Bath has to offer – you might find yourself pondering the question: to brie, or not to brie? The answer's obvious, which is why we're eternally thankful for the lovely café situated next door. It's the same business, so it's all high quality stuff, but they're not just cheesy lovers – they do a nice line in cakes and ice cream too. Plus the pear juice is so good it feels like a muscular angel just crushed a pear tree right over your face.

☺ *Mon–Fri, 9.30am–5.30pm;*
Sat, 9am–5.30pm

🍴 *Crayfish and rocket sandwich, £4.50*

Jazz Café

1 Kingsmead Square

(01225) 329 007

Jazz Café is one of three establishments on Kingsmead vying for a dip into your moneybag, but you could do worse than choose to lunch here. Fine outdoor seating and a smart interior dishing up quality nosh for a few bob. It fits in between the quality and price schemes of The Waverley and Boston Tea Party, as does its location, but it trumps them both with a booze licence, a real up yours to their competitors, allowing you to hang free like some crazy kind of hepcat over bebop and acid trumpet honks. Or just get drunk to jazz if you'd rather.

☺ *Mon–Sat, 8am–9pm; Sun, 10.30am–4pm*

🍴 *Double full English, £5*

Guildhall Market Café

Guildhall Market

(01225) 461 593

Perhaps Jacques Chirac was right in a way. England may not be as renowned for our cuisine as the French. You could say that fish and chips looks bland next to moules frites. Perhaps cassoulet is better than beans on toast. What we're saying is we don't care. La cuisine française just doesn't cut it when you sit it next to a perfectly formed plate of ham, egg and chips. How can you compare a croissant or a pain au chocolat to a full fry-up? You can't. So get here, sit yourself down at a Formica table and get a bit of English in you. Proper English.

☺ *Mon–Sat, 9am–4pm*

🍴 *Ham, egg and chips, £3.95*

Le Parisien

Shires Yard

(01225) 447 147

Being one of the best outdoor courtyards in Bath, this place should by rights be packed with elegant French women looking aloof, as distress-finish Gallic males mull over philosophical issues while sipping small coffees. Unfortunately it's mostly packed with loud American tourists and hopeful day trippers. Still, with a bit of self-delusion, you can ignore the brash clientele and above-average prices to have an enjoyable meal of vaguely French cuisine in a lovely setting. The fact that they sell Orangina in those funny little glass bottles helps, too.

☺ *Mon–Sat, 8am–5.30pm; Sun, 9am–5pm*

🍴 *Croque monsieur, £5.25*

Riverside Café

17 Argyle Street

(01225) 480 532

It's up there with the best views in Bath, with al fresco seating looking out at Pultney Bridge and on over the Avon. Unfortunately, it's less than likely you'll see any of it with the number of tourists waggling their fat arses in your face, heads poking out over the railings. Being forced inside by stampedes is no bad thing though, with a wide selection of breakfast, lunch and dinner, all cooked to mouth-watering perfection. Watch out for their tempting wine list – if you don't smash your head on the low ceilings, then do tread carefully when you get back next to the river.

🕒 *Sun–Wed, 9am–5pm; Thu–Sat, 9am–9pm*

🍴 *Enchiladas, £7.20*

Waverly Café

4 New Street

(01225) 462 553

When the Georgian stone and toffs get a bit much, get down here for a bit of real life. Forget organic eggs and farmers' market sausages, the Waverly makes a proper full English, battery hens and all. It's proper lorry driver treats, fried and slapped on a plate – expect chips with everything. And please don't ask for granola. You'll be dining with a few bruisers with prison tattoos and possibly a man who makes his own paper hats, but you'll fit in fine, as long as you don't start acting up. Don't say we didn't warn you.

🕒 *Mon–Sat, 7.30am–5.30pm;*

Sun, 10am–4pm

🍴 *Basic full English, £3.75*

Eat

RESTAURANTS

Aqua
88 Walcot Street
(01225) 471 371

Water, the stuff of life. It can cause death though in large quantities, which links us to the décor, which is borderline overkill, or possibly one of the prettiest interiors in Bath. We are undecided. What we have decided on is that it is a massive menu filled with pleasant sounding and pleasant tasting things. We did have reservations about it being on Walcot though. 'Um, waiter, there's a dreadlock in my soup.'

☺ *Sun–Thu, 11am–11pm;*
Fri–Sat, 11.30am–12pm
🍽 *Italian fish stew, £10.50*
💰 *£13.95*

Bottelinos
5 Bladud Building
(01225) 464 861

It's Itchy's job to overindulge. Our belly is growing by the minute. Anyone in the same position should use our task and reward system. Exert yourself and you get a treat. Climbing the hill to this little restaurant gets you one of the best lunchtime menus in Bath. Pasta and great veggie options aside, the pizzas are the best in Bath, giant discs of joy for a few pounds. Overindulge while you're here. There's always the walk back down to make up for it.

☺ *Mon–Sat, 12pm–2.30pm & 5.30pm–11pm;*
Sun, 12pm–7pm
🍽 *Napoletana, £7.25 (lunch special, any pizza or pasta £4.95)*
💰 *£11.50*

Ask
George Street
(01225) 789 997

There are an awful lot of clichés about mediocrity. 'Middle of the road', 'Dull as dishwater', and 'As interesting as watching paint dry': these are just the tip of the iceberg. Why so many recycled phrases about averageness? We blame Ask. Aside from this Italian bar/restaurant's astonishing averageness, it's part of a chain whose brethren are so uniform all they're missing is a logoed baseball cap. In the face of all these identically undistinguished venues, is it any wonder people use the same description over and again?

☺ *Mon–Sun, 12pm–11pm*
🍽 *Chicken calzone, £8.45*
💰 *£11.95*

Browns
Orange Grove
(01225) 461 199

This restaurant/bar is situated in what used to be the old court house, but Browns has yet to discover how to make the old jailhouse rock. Maybe it's as simple as turning up the treble on the droning music system, maybe it's just that every pie with a lid added or every fishcake with mash looks like something is missing from the plate. It's all very sterile and average, which is a shame, but not yet a crime. Elvis has left the building... still hungry.

☺ *Mon–Sat, 10am–11pm; Sun, 11am–10.30pm; food, Mon–Fri, 12pm–10.30pm;*
Sat–Sun, 11am–10pm
🍽 *Duck confit, £12.75*
💰 *£11.50*

□ ■ □ □ □ □ □ □ □ □ □ □

Beaujolais

5 Chapel Row

(01225) 423 417

If you know your claret from your Beaujolais you'll make no mistake with this gorgeous bistro in the centre of the city. The lively, cosmopolitan atmosphere and exquisite modern European cuisine (all locally produced and sourced) makes for a wonderfully fine dining experience. Be sure to show off your vintellect and order from the owners' speciality wine list. Charmless? Not us.

🕒 *Mon–Tue, 5.30pm–9.30pm; Wed–Thu, 10pm–2.30pm & 5.30pm–9.30pm; Fri–Sat, 9am–2.30pm & 5.30pm–10pm*

🍴 *Pan-fried fillet of black bream, caramelised salsify and vanilla mussel butter, 13.50*

💷 **£13**

Situated on Bath's Chapel Row, ***Beaujolais Bistro Bar*** has long enjoyed a reputation for serving up some of the finest cuisine found in the South West.

5 chapel row (by queen square)
bath. ba1 1hn
phone: 01225 423417
www.beaujolaisbath.co.uk

Eat

Chequers

50 Rivers Street

(01225) 360 017

An Itchy favourite, Chequers is the best gastropub in town. Talented French chefs serve up the most delectable gastrogrub known to man, with superb roasts on Sundays and outside tables if you fancy a spot of al fresco dining in the summer. No mention of Tesco here. They have a great selection of local real ales, including Bath Gem, the jewel in an already sparkling crown. Hire out your own private dining room for ultimate decadence.

🕒 *Mon–Thu, 5pm–11pm; Fri–Sat, 12pm–11.30pm; Sun, 12pm–10.30pm*

🍴 *Salmon fillet served with coriander egg noodles and lime pickle yoghurt, £18.50*

💷 *£12.50*

Demuth's Vegetarian

2 North Parade Passage

(01225) 446 059

The place for every protein-deficient veggie to drag their withering body. A couple of decades at the top of Bath's leafy food chain means there's much more on offer here than the usual veg risotto/veg tart combo. They make vegetables taste so good that even the most hard-line carnivore will concede that you don't need slabs of animal flesh to make things tasty. Itchy feels silly now, smuggling in that bit of meat in a hankie. Just make sure you dispose of it quietly.

🕒 *Mon–Fri & Sun, 10am–10pm; Sat, 9am–10pm; Sun, 10am–10pm*

🍴 *Mediterranean meze, £12.95*

💷 *£14.50*

Eastern Eye

8a Quiet Street

(01225) 422 323

They've had the awards, they've got the dishes, the staff are unbelievably lovely and the architecture is enough to make a grown man stand in awe in the middle of the dining room until he's asked to move to his seat. Along with some of the finest curries in Bath, the menu boasts a handy little system to tell you just how hot your curry is. Very handy for those competitive sorts out there who end up sweating all over their meals and gasping conversation at you from over the table just to prove they can take it.

🕒 *Mon–Sun, 12pm–12.30pm & 6pm–11.30pm*

🍴 *Chicken jalfrezi, £7.70*

💷 *£12.95*

F.east

5–10 James Street West

(01225) 333 500

You know the drill. It's a Chinese buffet. Punters like circus acts, balancing impossible amounts of food onto plates smaller than a fist, possibly in both hands, and another on their foot, with everyone competing to see how much they can get away with before the laws of physics take control. There are 60 dishes here, which adds up to a lot of balancing acts and a lot of people going green in the face and large in the belly.

🕑 *Mon–Thu, 12pm–3pm & 6pm–10.30pm; Fri, 12pm–3pm & 6pm–11pm; Sat, 12pm–4pm & 5pm–11pm; Sun, 12pm–4pm & 6pm–10.30pm*

🍴 *Lunch, £6.50; dinner, £12.50*

The Firehouse Rotisserie

2 John Street

(01225) 482 070

From a restaurant that's supposedly Californian, we were expecting to do shit like 'hanging loose' or picking up meals made entirely by the hands of pretentious nouvelle pricks. What we actually got are big pieces of meat and fusion cooking that actually worked for the most part, which is a triumph in itself. So it's a little bit pretentious, but maybe pretentious like a good old pretentious art house film, not one of those modern ones where people just sit in a room naked, hooting like chimps and turning the light on and off.

🕑 *Mon–Sat, 12pm–2.30pm & 6pm–11pm*

🍴 *Half rotisserie chicken, £11.95*

💷 *£12.95*

Fishworks

6 Green Street

(01225) 448 707

Itchy stood outside so long once, people started putting change by our feet. The downstairs fishmongers attracts us like the windows of sweet shops do small children. So many treats on offer, from bottom feeders to the finest quality bass and squid. The upstairs restaurant puts this fishy fare on plates with fantastic adornments. As if this wasn't enough, they'll cook up anything in the shop for you, regardless of whether it's on the menu or not. Cod, we love this plaice.

🕑 *Mon–Sat, 12pm–3pm & 5pm–11pm*

🍴 *Sea bream baked with herbs and Riesling, £14.95*

💷 *£11.95*

Ha! Ha! Bar and Canteen

The Tramshed, Beehive Yard

(01225) 421 200

Ha! Ha! may be in every city ever, but this one happens to be right next to the train station. Arguably a bar for train spotters then, this place is worth hanging your anorak in. Situated in the bohemian back tracks of Bath, it's clinical-looking and stands out like a nun in a brothel, but the food is good and reasonably priced, and the smokers are kept warm and happy outside under the heated terrace. Definitely a nice place to stoke up your engine. Now, where's that nun?

🕑 *Sun–Wed, 10am–11pm; Thu–Sat, 10am–12am*

🍴 *Rack of lamb, £11.75*

💷 *£10.95*

Eat

Hudson Bar & Grill

14 London Street

(01225) 332 323

It's a reasonably cool and grown up place this. Maybe too expensive by a couple of quid, but it keeps the riff raff out on the streets where they belong. Far be it for us to judge, but sometimes a fellow just needs a nice drink surrounded by a few 30 somethings, or a menu that's a little bit contemporary and a kitchen that actually cooks things properly, like steaks bigger-than-your-average, and certainly better-than-most. On the odd occasions we can actually afford it, we feel all cool and grown up.

⏰ *Mon–Sat, 5pm–11pm;*
food, 6pm–10.30pm

🍴 *12oz ribeye, £17.50*

La Tasca

36 Broad Street

(01225) 466 477

First impressions: cubist Picasso meets abstract Rothko. Get us. How cultured are we? Basically it's like sitting in a modern art gallery to eat your dinner. Ok, so it's one of a chain of seven, but good chains are best left unbroken. The tapas is good. One is a snack, two is a meal and three is being plain greedy. The closest you'll get to Spain this side of the channel, and without a sun lounger-grabbing German or sick, mangy donkey in sight. Brilliant. Best book for the evenings, mind.

⏰ *Mon–Sat, 12pm–11pm;*
Sun, 12pm–10.30pm

🍴 *Prawns with garlic mayonnaise, £4.35*

✅ *£11.75*

Jamuna

9–10 High Street

(01225) 464 631

Itchy dropped a fork here and two waiters almost broke the Olympic 100 metres record to pick it up and replace it. The service borders on the subservient but Itchy likes to be spoiled occasionally. Your efforts climbing up the many stairs to the restaurant will be rewarded with a great view of Bath Abbey; with or without the curry louts. There's very little to add other than great food, great prices, great place. Can you remember when India last won an Olympic Medal? If only there was an egg and spoon event.

⏰ *Mon–Sun, 12pm–2.30pm & 6pm–12am*

🍴 *Chicken tikka bhuna, £8.25*

✅ *£11.95*

Las Iguanas

12 Seven Dials, Sawclose

(01225) 336 666

Between the salsa in the speakers and the plantains on the plate, it's a theme restaurant that doesn't skimp on the Latin extravagance. Tortillas, fajitas and other spicy delicacies are all served up under bright lights and showy decoration. There's a courtyard outside and a cocktail bar downstairs if you haven't supped on enough rum cocktails, (is there such a thing as enough rum cocktails?). The mojitos are so good they made Itchy want to move to a favela and play football in bare feet.

⏰ *Mon–Thu, 12pm–11pm; Fri–Sat,*
12pm–11.30pm; Sun, 12pm–10.30pm

🍴 *Xinxim, £9.80*

✅ *£12.50*

Le Flamma

7 Edgar Buildings

(01225) 433 900

Alsatian food, far from what we expected, is quite the delicacy. The Alsace speciality on offer here is far from variety meats in jelly. They're called tartes flambés, and they're jolly little quiche-style savoury tarts, a pleasure on the palate and surprisingly well-priced. The theme continues – regional French classics at very reasonable prices. Wash it down with wine from their own vineyard, or order something in from the extensive champagne list. Get the lead out, we're going walkies tonight darling.

🕒 *Mon–Sat, 10am–late;*
Sun, 10am–5pm
🍴 *Daube of beef, £11.95*
💷 *£11.95*

The Olive Tree

4–7 Russell Street

(01225) 447 928

When you've upset the other half, this is a good place to offer the olive branch of peace, or perhaps just use it to beat a bit of sense back into them, because you're going to need to have shares in quite a successful olive press business to get the most out of the menu here. If you have pockets big enough, then you can enjoy a fine night out of fine wines, peaceful interiors and ridiculously well-thought out, and well-executed dishes.

🕒 *Mon, 7pm–10pm; Tue–Sat, 12pm–2pm*
& 7pm–10pm; Sun, 12.30pm–2pm &
7pm–10pm
🍴 *Roasted lamb and sweetbreads, £18.50*
💷 *£15*

Moon and Sixpence

6a Broad Street

(01225) 460 962

The prices mean that those of us whose faces don't tend towards a horsey indication of inbreeding will sadly only be able to experience this place's lovely little plates of food on special occasions. Indeed, it was the site of one of Itchy's finest anniversary meals. The fact that the romance dissolved into hatred is almost certainly in no way down to the venue. If you lack the cash of the polo-loving punters, you can always opt for the fantastic wine bar here to make visits more regularly.

🕒 *Mon–Sat, 12pm–2.30pm & 5.30pm–*
10.30pm; Sun, 6pm–10.30pm
🍴 *Duck breast with rosti, £16.50*
💷 *£12.95*

Eat

Panahar

8 Moorland Road

(01225) 471 999

If heaven is a foot massage from Deirdre Barlow, then follow Itchy's feet to Bath's equivalent of *Coronation Street*. Like Deirdre, Moorland Road is ugly, but behind the saggy tits beats the jewel of a heart that is Panahar. The food is absolutely delicious, served by staff that will go onto your Christmas card list and you can bring your own booze from the offy along the road. Perfect for those of us that could do with keeping the cost overdraft-friendly. You've just got to get past those legendary huge glasses.

🕒 *Mon–Sun, 12pm–2pm & 5.30pm–11pm*

🍴 *Chicken masala, £6.20*

🍷 *BYO*

Pizza Hut

1–3 Westgate Buildings

(01225) 448 586

Alright, so it's not the best pizza restaurant in the city. Possibly it's not even the best pizza restaurant located at 1–3 Westgate Buildings. Yes, the pizzas will arrive nuked beyond recognition, and the soft drinks will inevitably be overly sweet and flat – if you send them back, the only difference will be that the waiting staff will have slightly more contempt in their scowl next time. However, you just cannot beat the value of their lunchtime pizza buffet. For £4.50 all-you-can-eat, you can cram three days' food into one lunchtime. Ace.

🕒 *Mon–Sun, 11am–11pm*

🍴 *Pizza only buffet, £4.99*

🍷 *£9.99*

Pasta Galore

31 Barton Street

(01225) 463 861

The name's terrible, the inside hasn't changed since the 70s (nor have most of the clientele), but despite the fact it feels a little like walking into your grandparents' wake, there's a tatty charm there. Freshly made pasta, classic and not-so-classic sauces, all well-executed, all at prices that won't dent your pension. However innocent old people might seem, they are devious little secret keepers that trick us away from decent food with their corpse-like visages. Damn them all.

🕒 *Sun–Wed, 12pm–2.30pm & 6pm–10.30pm; Thu–Sat, 12pm–2.30pm & 6pm–11pm*

🍴 *Lamb stew with tagliatelle, £7.50*

🍷 *£10.20*

Pria Balti

4a Argyle Street

(01225) 462 323

Sister restaurant to Rajpoot, Pria is the younger and uglier of the two, but by no means without its virtues. It's hard to see them in respect of Rajpoot's overwhelming beauty, but it's got those hidden qualities, the kind you don't get at face value. The food isn't quite as good, the service lacks that edge, but it's there for you when you need it. Open 'til 2am at the weekends, and with that laid back aspect you wish its sister would occasionally have, sometimes it's worth going for the bit of rough.

🕒 *Sun–Thu, 6.30pm–1.30am; Fri–Sat, 6.30pm–2am*

🍴 *Chicken balti, £5.95*

🍷 *£8.20*

The Pump Rooms

Abbey Churchyard

(01225) 444 477

Call us crazy, but we half expected the Roman Baths' restaurant to be serving up historically accurate food. However, with the number of people of that era winding up with gout, rickets or some other crippling illness, we can see why they plump for a modern menu. Best is the afternoon tea, with dainty treats served up on tiered silver platters. But be warned: the price'll have you choking on your cucumber sandwich (minus the crusts, obviously).

🕒 *Mon–Sun, morning menu, 9.30am–12pm; lunch, 12pm–2.30pm; afternoon tea, 2.30pm–4.30pm*

🍴 *Traditional pump room tea, £15.50*

💰 *£15*

Tilleys

3 North Parade Passage

(01225) 484 200

Things Itchy likes about Tilleys: it's French but it doesn't stand on ceremony, and the food is very tasty indeed. Things Itchy doesn't like about Tilleys: the portions are so small that it's basically a tapas restaurant. With dishes in small, medium and large sizes, the idea is that you order multiple plates. It's a clever ploy, because there are so many good dishes on offer that you'll want more than one anyway. And maybe even more than the two they recommend. If only the prices were as small as the portions...

🕒 *Mon–Sat, 12pm–2.30pm & 6.30pm–10.30pm*

🍴 *Escargots à la Bourguignonne, £6*

💰 *£12*

Rajpoot

4 Argyle Street

(01225) 464 758

It might seem expensive if you're used to the cost of your local takeaway, but you're paying for quality. Fantastic ingredients make fantastic food and three differently styled dining areas make fantastic surroundings. Plus, fantastic service – they employ someone just to open the door for you on entrance – means it's worth the extra. Even if you do find something bad to say about it, we wouldn't, because 'Rajpoot' refers to a warrior race. Watch the way they handle those tandoori skewers.

🕒 *Sun–Thu, 12pm–2.30pm & 6pm–11pm; Fri–Sat, 12pm–2.30pm & 6pm–11.30pm*

🍴 *Tandoori Thali, £14.50*

💰 *£12.95*

Eat

The Wheatsheaf

Combe Hay

(01225) 833 504

Alright, you're either in for a bit of a drive or a half marathon through dense country, but get here and you'll find the perfect weekend pub. One of those pubs you take a paper down to and get set up for the day. Heap perfection on top in the form of Sunday roasts, which are both massive and yum yum, and then add another helping for the breakfasts, which have been spreading word faster than teen scumbags spread chlamydia. Very fast and very delicious. The service/food that is, not the chlamydia.

🕙 Tue–Sun, 12pm–2.30pm & 6.30pm–9.30pm (Tue–Thu) & 6.30pm–10pm (Fri–Sat)

🍴 Fillet of Aberdeen Angus beef, £21

💰 £12.95

Yak Yeti Yak

12a Argyle Street

(01225) 442 299

Be daring. They've got chairs here, but give you the chance to eat traditionally on scatter cushions and low tables. If you're back's as weak as crepe paper, avoid it, but otherwise it does make the meal more exotic and authentic. The food's familiar but different. It's Indian curry-ish, but here they use spices to flavour the food, not burn your teeth to stumps. They really have recreated a little bit of Nepal here, down to the Himalaya-like descent to and ascent from this subterranean treasure.

🕙 Mon–Thu & Sun, 12pm–2pm & 6pm–10pm; Fri–Sat, 12pm–2pm & 6pm–10.30pm

🍴 Masuko jhol, £6.90

💰 £11.50

Yum Yum Thai

17 Kingsmead Square

(01225) 445 253

At last, a Thai restaurant that doesn't try to play up to our stereotyped view of what an oriental eatery should be. There are no gaudy trinkets, no buffets packed with jam-covered meats, and no ludicrously red décor. Instead, they serve classic Thai dishes in a minimalist setting with good service from happy staff. If you ask Itchy, this place is better than establishments with finer food. Call us picky, but we prefer to eat without being watched over by giant brass elephants in the corner.

🕙 Mon–Sat, 12pm–2.30pm & 6pm–11pm; Sun, 6pm–11pm

🍴 Quick Thai rice, £5.95

💰 £12

Drink

Drink

Welcome to Drink

Bath is definitely in the running for the UK title of 'most pubs per square inch', but Itchy has done the 'hard work' of separating quality from quantity for you. Our favourite three places to sink a pint have got to be...1) **The Salamander (3 John Street, 01225 428 889)** for a relaxed atmosphere and décor that has withstood the army of chrome currently invading the nation's pubs... 2) **The Old Green Tree (12 Green Street, 01225 329 314)** for the choicest ales and a tempting selection of Belgian beers... And finally, 3) **The Lamb & Lion (15 Lower Borough Walls, 01225 474 931)** – great for drinks deals that include something infinitely more palatable than a WKD or a warm Carling. Hurry on down there. Now we've let the cat out of the bag, these places are going to be heaving. That's the kind of influence we exert.

Itchy's top five venues for drinking cocktails in Bath

1. Sub 13, 4 Edgar Buildings
(01225 466 667)
2. Lambrettas,
8–10 North Parade
(01225 464 650)
3. Sam Weller's,
14 Upper Borough Walls
(01225 474 911)
4. Pulp, 38 Monmouth Streeet
(01225 466 411)
5. Karanga, 8–10 Manvers Street
(01225 316 198)

CENTRAL

B A R

A bar and cafe in one, embodies quality and warmth.
It is the third place, between work and home;
created for you to enjoy.

Open for breakfast from 10 am,
serving a full seasonal lunch menu,
and an evening tapas menu.

10 Upper Borough Walls • Bath • BA1 1RG
01225 333 939
www.centralbarbath.co.uk

Drink

BARS

Adventure Café and Bar

5 Princes Buildings, George Street

(01225) 462 038

We would say we probably love it as much as we love our auntie, but not as much as our mum. Not metaphorically. It runs that deep. As deep as our love for blood relations. When lunch and dinner come to an end, the music sparks and the lights get lower, filling the place out with all sorts of pretty young things. A wide range of booze and eclectic music taste keeps this place interesting. Happily, it never gets too much though; it's just all too calm and collected.

Ⓒ *Mon–Wed, 10am–5pm; Thu–Sat, 10am–12am; Sun, 10am–11pm*

Blue Rooms

George Street

(01225) 470 040

A touch classy this place, and definitely at the high end of the Bath bars. There's three bars to fulfil various needs, with a busy main bar, a relaxed one out the back and a music room with a DJ thrown in. It isn't a spit and sawdust shithole like some of the other places about – there's plenty of them if that's your thing – so get your decent boots on, boys and girls, and some kind of sparkly top. Their website says it's somewhere for everyone, and that's true enough... If you're 30 or 40 and single, and have money, but you can sneak in if you've got an old face and that.

Ⓒ *Mon–Thu, 7pm–2am; Fri, 7pm–3am; Sat, 7pm–4am*

Central Bar

10 Upper Borough Walls

(01225) 333 939

With a cocktail menu longer than one of your grandad's war stories, staff at Central relish the challenge of whizzing together any kooky concoction you can dream up. Try their birthday punch bowls for special occasions. A decent music policy of breaks, electro and funky house provide the soundtrack to your evening, with DJs at weekends spinning funk and soul classics. The food ain't bad either, with tasty dishes served up for breakfast, lunch and dinner. And with a function room available for free hire, this place does the full monty.

Ⓒ *Sun–Thu, 10am–11pm; Fri–Sat, 10am–2am*

Ⓘ *Goat's cheese crostini and salad, £6.25*

Ⓐ *Cocktails, £6*

Delfter Krug

Saw Close

(01225) 443 352

By night Delfter Krug is Bath's sharp superclub, offering up a stellar serving of great music. There's no question that it's an exquisite and integral part of Bath's nightlife. But don't despair in the waking hours – by day it operates as a smart and stylish bar. With its great reputation and incredible drinks promos every week of the year, DK continues to dole out decent food and booze to many satisfied (and merry) customers. This is a well-established and well-run venue, a dead cert for a great day/ evening/night out. There's even an outside seating area. Now that's a full house, folks.

© Mon–Thu, 12pm–2am; Fri–Sat, 12pm–3am

© £11

GREAT FOOD SERVED ALL DAY

- Delfter Krug, Sawclose, Bath 01225 443352
  (Opposite Theatre Royal)
- www.delfterkrug.com
- Open from midday 'til late 7 days/nights a week

www.itchybath.co.uk

31

Grappa Bar

3 Belvedere, Lansdown Road

(01225) 448 890

If you're tired of being served cocktails so bad they make you want to get behind the bar and mix one yourself, you need to go to Grappa. A stunning bar in the heart of upper town, you'll be served tip top cocktails by trained professionals. As the name suggests, they know their grappa and have an extensive list of wines and champagnes too, all served by the glass. And to stop you getting too tipsy from all that tipple, order some delicious antipasti or a stone-baked pizza to keep you on the straight and narrow. The service is top notch to boot.

🕐 *Mon–Sat, 5pm–11pm; Sun, 6pm–10.30pm*

💷 *£12.95*

Sub 13

4 Edgar Buildings, George Street

(01225) 466 667

Some places are considered so cool that even if the ugliest and dullest kids you know so much as mention their name they are deemed cool by association. Super-chic, über-classy Sub 13 is one such place. Spend an evening here sipping on champagne and expertly prepared cocktails. With a contemporary bar area, vaults, a sub-basement hideaway and a patio where sizzling BBQ food is served up in the summer, there's plenty of places to set up shop for the day/ night. Hell, we'd live here if we could – thank God it's available for private hire.

🕒 *Mon–Sun, 5pm–12pm*

🍹 *Basil and honey daiquiri, £6.50*

Sample Cocktail
Pomegranate Blush £6.50
mint, fresh pomegranate
ginger beer & vodka

Contact Info
01225 46 66 67
email:drinks@sub13.net
www.sub13.net

Opening Times
Monday - Saturday
5pm - 12am
Private hire available on Sundays

"Baths uber cool and super chic underground bar"

Drink

Revolutions
George Street,
(01225) 336 145

You'd probably guess from the six-foot stickers in the window that it's a bar specialising in vodka. And you'd be right. Here, you can sup on premium imported vodkas, standards in silly flavours or over a hundred cocktails. Most people enjoy it by simply bingeing on the cheap stuff, which makes sense, given that the effect is the same, however much you pay. Two floors, countless pretty punters and a good pre-club atmosphere make up for the fact that this place is about as Russian as Ivan Drago from *Rocky IV*.

🕔 *Mon–Sun, 10.30am–12am; food,*
Mon–Sun, 11am–9pm
💷 *With privilege card, £8*

Gascoyne Place
1 Sawclose Place
(01225) 445 854

We were all excited by the prospect of multiple Paul Gascoigne analogies to explain the class and depth of this fine establishment until we realised they've only gone and spelt their names differently. Now where's the fun in the that? No one's ever even heard of Paul Gascoyne. We suppose you could get someone to read it out for you if you wanted, because they're pronounced exactly the same. Yeah, pass it over to someone now. Read from here: Even Paul Gascoigne couldn't find anything to cry about at this place. Pass it back: Oh. That wasn't really worth it was it?

🕔 *Mon–Wed,11am–12am; Thu–Sat,*
11am–1am; Sun, 12pm–11.30pm

The Common Room
2 Saville Road
(01225) 425 550

A bit lacking on the imagination front, we checked the dictionary for the word 'common' to see if we could play on it in this review to comic or ingenious effect. 16 entries. We couldn't. Often occurring or frequently seen? Nope. It's well hidden away. Belonging to the community as a whole? Nope. It's members or entry charge at the weekend. Of the standard that most people expect? Nope. It's really lovely in here – a fine décor, good crowd, the music fits. Considered to be ill-bred or vulgar? Never. See common stock? What does that entry even mean?

🕔 *Mon–Wed, 6pm–1am; Thu–Sat, 6pm–2am*
💷 *£12*

Drink

PUBS

The Ale House

1 York Street
(01225) 400 088

The downstairs has always smelt a little too awful for our liking, and we can never make up our minds whether it's the location and state of their sanitary facilities, or the sizeable elderly contingent who populate said cellar. That aside, you can get a meal and a bottle of wine for a tenner so who really cares? We would add that upstairs it's full of hard-line committed drunks who make us smile a lot. They are all lovely, even though if you listen very carefully, you can hear their kidneys screaming.

Ⓒ Mon–Sat, 11am–11pm;
Sun, 12pm–10.30pm

The Boater

9 Argyle Street
(01225) 464 211

With three floors – one for the locals, one for the pool tables and one for the youngsters – and the biggest beer garden in Bath, if not the whole of the West Country, The Boater gets surprisingly close to being full at the weekend. Not least due to the fact that it offers drooling fanboys of the oval ball the opportunity to drool over the occasional visit from Bath rugby players. Add to this the lavish summer barbecues in the garden, regular pub football tournaments and proximity to one of the best views of the weir that the city has to offer, and you'll understand its popularity.

Ⓒ Mon–Sat, 11am–11pm;
Sun, 12pm–10.30pm

The Assembly Inn

16–17 Alfred Street
(01225) 333 639

This place is student-friendly with big windows, so you can look outside and wonder how you managed to be in a place which is so depressingly average when there's plenty of other boozers for you to drink your money away in. And then you'll probably think, 'Oh look how far uphill I walked to come here, what a waste of my time and energy'. And finally you might hit upon a brilliant idea like, 'If places have massive windows, maybe I should look inside first to make sure that all of its patrons don't seem as if they're on the verge of hanging themselves.'

Ⓒ Mon–Thu, 11am–11.30pm; Fri–Sat, 11am–1am; Sun, 12pm–10.30pm

The Boathouse

Newbridge Road
(01225) 482 584

Picture the scene. You and your other half take a walk down the river on a pleasant summer's day. You come to a beer garden and sit, whispering sweet sonnets to each other while you enjoy a drink and a pub lunch. It's tasty and reasonably priced. The sunset tickles the tips of the Avon. Swans waddle among the tables. Summer perfection. Until you realise you'll be walking several miles home in the dark. In flip-flops. And it's cold. Come prepared.

Ⓒ Mon–Sat, 11am–11pm;
Sun, 12pm–10.30pm
Ⓜ Mushroom and goats
cheese lasagne, £7.95
Ⓐ £11

Drink

Cork & Bottle

11–12 Westgate Buildings

(01225) 330 470

Every pub has a crisis point some time or another. We never knew they could change their sexuality though. This is an ex-gayish pub taken over by Marstons brewery, which may strike you as a bit of a strange switch. Out with the pop and preening, and in with the bitter and big-screen sports. It's all pretty standard brewery fare, but with a bit of exotic tapas thrown in for good measure, plus wraps and all that kind of stuff to help keep your belly from your backbone. Pleasant then, and certainly not awful, but hardly a revolution in drinking venues.

☺ *Mon–Wed, 12pm–12am; Thu–Sat, 12pm–2am; Sun, 3pm–10.30pm*

Flan O Brien's

21 Westgate Street

(01225) 312 914

To avoid the same old clichés, we won't bother telling you that this is where to come for a good pint of Guinness. Or right bloody craic. And we won't say that you'll be lord of the dance or cavorting with leprechauns or all over the bar screaming *Danny Boy*. We'll just tell you instead that this is a genuine Irish pub, and incredibly popular too. With a late-night bar, Sky Sports on the big screen and an extensive range of beers, wines and single malt Irish whiskeys, this place is more than worth the nine-to-five shrapnel, especially on a Tersday.

☺ *Mon–Tue, 12pm–11pm; Wed–Fri & Sun, 12pm–late; Sat, 11am–late*

✪ *Pint of Guinness, £3.05*

The Crystal Palace

10–11 Abbey Green

(01225) 482 666

A crystal palace may be a brittle structure, but thankfully, this one was built on firm foundations: 300 year-old foundations. It might have changed hands a few times, but it's been open that long for a reason. It's fronted by a quaint little square and backed by a sheltered beer garden, and in between is a solid bar with a smooth atmosphere and decent service. You may have an aversion to the place if you hate the football team of the same name, but otherwise it's a decent choice. Here's to another 300 years (you'll have to imagine us raising a glass for this to work).

☺ *Mon–Sat, 11am–11pm; Sun, 12pm–10.30pm*

The Hop Pole

7 Albion Buildings, Upper Bristol Road

(01225) 446 327

One of the prettiest gardens in Bath helps make this one of the city's finest pubs. All the better for being well outside of the city centre, it's worth a walk for the ales on tap alone. Add to this a great bar menu and an even better restaurant attached out back, and anyone who doesn't know about this place is a lesser person for it. Those who do are so enthusiastic about it that Itchy's even thinking about setting up a competition to see if we can find anybody in the city with a bad word to say about this place. Though we're not optimistic about finding any.

☺ *Mon–Sat, 11am–11pm; Sun, 12pm–10.30pm*

The Garricks Head

8 St Johns Place

(01225) 318 368

We first started coming here on the off chance we might pick up some Uncle Monty style benefactor, who's a bit creepy in a way, but won't actually make you do anything for money, so he's alright. Then we noticed we were coming back for different reasons. Even though it's attached to the theatre, The Garricks Head isn't all full of luvvies, and since the team behind the King William took over, the food here is obviously quite brilliant, and can be washed down with the finest wines known to humanity.

Ⓒ *Mon–Thu & Sun, 12pm–11pm; Fri–Sat, 12pm–12am; food, Mon–Sun, 12pm–3.30pm & 6pm–10.30pm*

The Hobgoblin

47 St James' Parade

(01225) 460 785

You'll know when you walk in if The Hobgoblin's the place for you. If it is, people will admire your boots and your tattoos. They might even pop over so you can compare adornments. If you're not a Hobgoblin guy or gal, everybody will stare at you relentlessly until you can't bear it anymore. They'll stare so hard you'll feel the impact of each glare like a weak slap, and you'll think of either bursting into tears, or fighting through it stubbornly, only to fall on the ground screaming, 'Why can't you accept me?' It's the sort of place where 'individuals' go to fit in.

Ⓒ *Mon–Thu, 12pm–12am; Fri–Sat, 12pm–1am; Sun, 12pm–11pm*

Drink

The Huntsman

1 Terrace Walk

(01225) 482 900

Like a superhero with an alter ego, by day it's an unassuming pub skulking in the shadow of the abbey. By night it fights against the injustice of standard closing times imposed by most pubs. It's not a superhero with cool claws and a surly but lovable personality like Wolverine, but more like Gambit, the professional thief who throws playing cards. Analogies aside, it stays open until two and there's a tiny dance floor upstairs full of nobody who says anything cool, but like Gambit, at least it tries. The Huntsman's likely to live happily very after with its own Rogue.

Mon–Sat, 11am–2am; Sun, 12pm–10pm

£9.50

The King of Wessex

James Street West

(01225) 303 380

At first, you think that everyone is surprisingly cheery, laughing, smiling, happy. But you'll soon realise that everyone's so smashed up on cheap booze that they can't even comprehend sentences, let alone complex metaphysical beings. It's a Wetherspoons, so it's full of people consuming gallons of alcohol and bland meals, but that's the charm. Or the charm could be the fact that you can go out with £20 and drink enough to put you in hospital but still afford a taxi home.

Mon–Sat, 9am–11.30pm; Sun, 9am–11pm; food, daily

10oz rump steak, £6.39

£7.99

The King William

36 Thomas Street

(01225) 428 096

If we had a section called 'Places that are a little bit special' in this guide, the King William would surely be in it. Since its transformation from a shitkicker pub, certain people have got all hot under the collar, saying things like 'Oh, this ain't a real pub, it's more like some restaurant or summink', Perhaps they do tend to emphasise the food here, but when it's good food, (and we mean really good food), then who cares about what people like that think?

Mon–Thu, 12pm–3pm & 5pm–11pm; Fri, 12pm–3pm & 5pm–12am; Sat, 12pm–12am; Sun, 12pm–11pm; food, Sun–Tue, 12pm–2.30pm; Wed–Sat, 12pm–2.30pm & 6pm–10pm

Belvedere Wine Vaults

25 Belvedere

(01225) 330 264

We really don't mind a refurbishment here and there, as long as it doesn't make a place worse. Since the takeover a couple of years ago this natty little bar has been going from strength to strength. Before, a lot of people hated it. Now a lot of people like it. We would say we like it too. Good booze, good food, nice atmosphere and the odd music night, with nothing letting it down but the monumental climb up the hill to get here. Also, possibly the massive injuries you would sustain if you tripped on the way home. You have to take risks if you want the rewards though.

Mon–Sat, 12pm–11pm; Sun, 12pm–10.30pm

Lamb and Lion

15 Lower Borough Walls

(01225) 474 931

Itchy is sad to announce the death of the 'extra large' choice of portion size. No more will we wrestle with the decision of three, six or nine sausages with our mash, or wonder how anyone could deal with those coma-inducing plates of meat. It leaves behind a brother 'large' and distant cousin 'regular'. They will continue being massive and cheap without him. We know he'll be happy up there, looking down on us necking booze deals, roughing it with the regulars and slowly blinding ourselves in the sun-trap garden. Rest in peace. Our waistlines will never be the same.

Mon–Sat, 11am–11pm;
Sun, 12pm–10.30pm

The Metropolitan

14 James Street West

(01225) 330 439

This used to be one of our favourite boozers before it got refurbished, just for the fact that it was dirty enough for no one to give a shit what you did, as long as you didn't wear anything too loud or act too exotically. Now it's been pasteurised and is part of the same chain as The Huntsman, so expect standard refurbishment boozer style, a few middle-agers and not much else. Someone go there and raise a toast to The Midland for us, will you? We've got better places to be now. And, now we come to think of it, so do you. What did you buy this book for, anyway? To come here? God, we hope not.

Mon–Sat, 12pm–12am; Sun, 12pm–10pm

Litten Tree

23 Milsom Street

(01225) 310 772

God knows how WKD have survived all these years. Perhaps the key to the lurid alcopop's success lies in the existence of this venue. Mainly full of sports students and meatheads quaffing the garish beverage, the Litten Tree is definitely for you if you enjoy shotgunning sweet drinks with a low alcoholic content while playing drinking games of a highly sexual bent with members of the same sex. If not, then the only way you'll enjoy an evening here is to arrive early and leave quickly. Unless you have a burning desire to watch people shout a lot and drink each other's urine for fun, that is.

Mon–Sun, 10am–11pm

Drink

O'Neills

1 Barton Street

(01225) 789 106

Fancy having another Irish pub in the same street as Flan's. Thankfully, this place is big enough to deal with the overspill from the majority of pubs come kick out time, which is its main usage, as they have a dance floor the size of four cocktail sticks arranged in a square and thus an excuse for a bit of late drinking and conversation. But then again, there's late licences cropping up all over the place now, so we don't want to say that it's completely redundant... but it's fair to say that it's not exactly setting the world alight with originality, flare and its scintillating personality either.

Mon–Sat, 12pm–2am;
Sun, 12pm–10.30pm

Pig and Fiddle

2 Saracen Street

(01225) 460 868

So popular that at the weekends the punters start to look like a mass of pink flesh and hair rather than a few people enjoying a drink, every inch of available space is taken up by someone having a good time. Luckily there's extra seating under umbrellas and heaters in the concrete garden, so you can still be a part of it if you find a spare corner of a chair or a paving slab to perch on. It's good here. Very good.

Mon–Sat, 11am–11pm; Sun, 12pm–10.30pm; food, Mon–Fri, 11am–7pm; Sat, 11am–6pm; Sun, 12pm–6pm

Mexicano burger (with choice of meat such as kangaroo and wild boar), £5.95

£11.75

The Old Green Tree

12 Green Street

(01225) 329 314

An actual pub. No flashing lights. No drinks promotions. No inoffensive house remixes. Pubs used to be about sitting in a room that wasn't your house and drinking. Apparently people didn't need distractions. Those that can deal with that get a huge choice of ales and Belgian beers, incredibly edible food and a bit of regulars' chatter. Bring a book in the day, or perhaps a friend, but don't go getting rowdy. You're going to sit and enjoy your booze like a grown up, aren't you now?

Mon–Sat, 11am–11pm; Sun, 12pm–10pm; food, Mon–Sat, 12pm–2.15pm

Sausage and mash, £8

£11

Rat and Parrot

38 Westgate Street

(01225) 461 642

Aptly named after its inhabitants: those rat-faced types who pipe on about the same old shit and make far too much racket. Maybe we're a little hard on the place, but we just don't like it, even though we think rats and parrots are pretty cool. Ironic huh? On the plus side, you could always try and gang up on the aforementioned people and keep them locked up from everyone else. But even with them locked away, it's still a grimy-looking pub with a terrible backing track which knocks out dirty cocktails and pints. They do have a really nice bouncer though.

Mon–Sat, 11am–11pm;
Sun, 12pm–10.30pm

Green Park Tavern
45 Lower Bristol Road
(01225) 400 050

With all the prime pub requirements, from
booze to food via sofas for a Sunday
snooze, you won't be disappointed by this
friendly and welcoming pub. Get together
with friends for a Sunday roast or a
Wednesday quiz, seven-ball them at pool
or out-fish the sharks at the poker table. In
a stroke of brilliance, the Green Park genii
have also brought a Wii to the pub, so you
can while away hours with a pint in one
hand and a teeny Wiiny wand in the other.
Those guys know that nobody is bad at
virtual bowling, even after a few pints.
Ultimate customer satisfaction guaranteed.
 Sun–Thu, 11am–12pm; Fri–Sat, 11am–2am
 £10

Drink

Porter Bar

2 Miles Buildings, George Street

(01225) 424 104

This place makes Itchy start to believe in creationism. If somewhere so complex can come out so perfect then surely we can accept that God made the universe. A pub that mixes bully beefs with dishevelled indie types and still keeps up a good atmosphere, with a basement bar downstairs putting on comedy, acoustic nights and DJs throughout the week. Throw in vegetarian food, painfully stylish staff, decent music, and the fact that it's next to Moles and it makes Itchy want to start spreading the gospel. Why not join us at 'prayer' here some time?

🕐 *Mon–Thu, 11.30am–12pm; Fri–Sat, 11.30am–1am; Sun, 12pm–11.30pm*

💰 *£11*

The Royal Oak

Lower Bristol Road

(01225) 481 409

An ale house through and through. It's a fair way out of town, but the walk is worth it if you're into a bit of bitter. Loads of pumps pouring out pints from micro-breweries across the land, they'll let you have a little taster to find the right ale for you. A busy Irish music night on Wednesdays is always good fun, and the locals here are welcoming as long as you don't ask for lager. The food's good too, but no steak and ale pie. Missed a trick there.

🕐 *Mon–Thu, 12pm–11pm; Fri–Sat, 12pm–12am; Sun, 12pm–10.30pm; food, Mon–Wed, 12pm–3pm; Thu–Fri, 12pm–3pm & 7pm–9pm; Sunday roasts, 12.30pm–3.30pm*

The Salamander

3 John Street

(01225) 428 889

Bath Ale have excelled themselves yet again. This fine addition to their pub conglomerate mixes old-fashioned pub sentiment with modern-day standards of hygiene, providing ample reason to while away your time drinking beer, not least because you won't get covered by a thin layer of dust or attract the attention of gruff locals, unlike some of Bath's other antique pubs. There's a decent supper room upstairs too, meaning that even the most cowardly chain pub attendee can finally feel like they fit in, without needing a dog on a bit of string or a tattoo on their neck.

🕐 *Mon–Thu, 11.30am–11pm; Fri–Sat, 11.30am–1am; Sun, 12pm–10.30pm*

The Saracen's Head

42 Broad Street

(01225) 426 518

Famous for being the pub where Charles Dickens wrote *The Pickwick Papers*, which is quite apt because at times the punters resemble Dickensian characters, not in the good way as loveable scamps with ragged clothes and dirty but angelic faces, but more like Bill Sykes and his dog, ready to pounce on you if you put a foot out of line. And keep your eyes on your purses and hands in your pockets just in case Fagin and his boys are lurking about. Whatever it was that made Dickens want to stay here back then, it certainly passed on around the same time he did.

◉ *Mon–Thu, 11am–11pm; Fri–Sat, 11am–1am; Sun, 12pm–10.30pm*

Velo Lounge

30 Moorland Road

(01225) 344 663

They've finally got a place for everyone in the student district to go locally and not be smashed up with fists or get disapproving looks. This place is pleasing to a lot of different people. Don't be massively surprised to be sitting on a bench at one end of the room looking at people drinking pints, mums meeting for coffees with prams in tow, and young folk being all wacky and ironic playing Battleships. All this at 10am; or any time really, anything goes. Decent food, decent drinks, attention to comfort, free wifi... the list goes on.

◉ *Mon–Sun, 9am–11pm*

🍴 *Grilled chicken burger, £6.95*

🍷 *£11.50*

The Star Inn

23 The Vineyards

(01225) 425 072

It is our opinion that there isn't anything like a proper old pub. It saddens us to see them slowly dying out in this age of cheap leather seating and fancy foreign cocktails. You just can't manufacture a place like The Star Inn. It's been created over an indeterminate period of time by thousands of men sitting around enjoying a ruddy pint and a fag, possibly some nuts, definitely some laughs. No transparently corporate decisions here. We don't want to lose places like these. They're like walking in comfortable old shoes; rarely exciting but always a pleasure and never a chore.

◉ *Mon–Sat, 11am–11pm; Sun, 12pm–10.30pm*

Volunteer Riflemans Arms

New Bond Street

(01225) 425 210

We can't help but think that there can't have been too many people willing to go out and shoot people on a volunteer basis when this pub was first conceived. But then again, we suppose it would make a bit more sense if they had been gun-toting midgets: then they would have been able to fit loads more in. Painfully small, but all the better for it, and with a close atmosphere created by a solid bunch of regulars, it's one of those places that you actually feel better for being in. We think people call it being quaint or something. We just think it's bloody good.

◉ *Mon–Thu, 11am–1am; Fri–Sat, 11am–2am; Sun, 12pm–11pm*

How to make your pint last all day

befriend the nearest person who looks like they might have full pockets. Drunk that one too? Tell someone you're about to become a parent. Necked that one as well? Well, there's no helping you then...

Play coin football – Fact: if you're not actually drinking, your drink lasts longer. Indulge in a nice game of coin footie instead. Place three coins in a triangle formation, then flick them forwards one by one, using the coin that's furthest back, sliding it between the other two. The target is the makeshift goal your opponent has made with his fingers

HARD UP, BUT LIKE NOTHING MORE THAN WHILING AWAY TIME IN A BOOZER? FEAR NOT. A TRIP TO THE PUB NEEDN'T BREAK THE BANK

Keep the pint cool – Get yourself one of those chemical ice-packs for injuries. After an hour or so, crack it open, and wrap it around your beverage. Hey presto: it's like you've just bought it.

Go minesweeping – Some people just don't understand the value of the last two sips. Wait 'til these wasteful types have left the pub, then nip over and finish their backwash. Take the glass to the bar afterwards, and the bar staff'll love you so much they'll let you carry on all day.

Create fake identities – Running perilously low on that pint? Quick, pretend it's your birthday and

Get a job there – Hey, we've given you four top tips already. What more do you want from us? If you can't make a pint last all day with these gems, you're going to have to ask the landlord for a job.

Illustration by Si Clarke

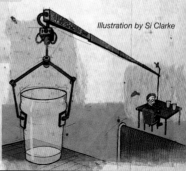

Dance

Right on Queue

Queue

DO YOU EVER FIND YOURSELF STANDING IN A LONG LINE TO ENTER A CLUB, GET A DRINK, OR GO FOR A PEE? THEN YOU'LL FIND ITCHY'S Q-TIPS ON WAYS TO AMUSE YOURSELF WHILE YOU HANG ABOUT WORTH THEIR WAIT IN GOLD

Get the party started before you even hit the floor. Just bring a bag of thick elastic bands to hand out to fellow queue-tey pies, and get everyone to pluck a different note. When you're at the bar, try blowing over the tops of bottles to entertain the other punters. If you're good enough, they might throw you enough loose change to pay for your drink.

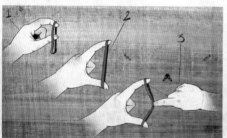

Before striding out, get down to the pound shop and buy a big bottle of the foulest perfume you can find, or even better, nip to a fishing shop and get your mitts on a bottle of lobster essence used for scenting baits. When waiting for a loo cubicle, pretend to be a toilet attendant, and offer exiting punters a free spritz of 'fragrance'. Every pongy person you zap with your minging musk is one fewer rival to compete against in the pulling stakes.

Or you can try the following trick. Start your evening at home by chowing down on beans and bhuna. Later, when you find yourself so far back in line that the folk at the front are in a different postcode, let the gas go. Watch the crowds shrink as they run from your stink, and try to figure out who it was who let rip. Don't strain too hard though, unless you fancy wandering home with the contents of your bowels sloshing around your smalls.

Illustration by Si Clarke

□ □ □ ■ □ □ □ □ □ □ □

Dance

CLUBS

Back To Mine
6 The Bladdud Building
(01225) 425 677

In the running for the venue with the most havoc-inducing name, be careful who you invite. Itchy has been attacked for being a sleaze many times. Though, granted, this bar was not neccessarily always the primary cause. We have also been caught here with the boot on the other foot and ended up here unexpectedly more than we'll admit. If you do get someone to come here with you, they'll be treated to a better kind of night out. There's no cheese, no kids stumbling about, and nobody dressing overtly like they have to get laid tonight.

● *Mon–Sat, 8.30pm–2am*

Club XL
90b Walcot Street
(01225) 464 241

Itchy isn't going to embellish this review. A pound a pint. That's the extent of the plus points covered in four words. The rest is a sweaty slum of a club, with Bath's filthier elements pounding their guts to death with shots and pints and stumbling to bad music. You get everything you expect, so it's fights, lots of bare flesh, vomiting on the dance floor, girls crying and ugly people fondling each other in corners that are nowhere near dark enough. It's the sort of place that really makes you worry about the human race. A rotten meat market, but it is pound a pint, so it's swings and roundabouts innit?

● *Times vary*

THE WORLD FAMOUS LIVE MUSIC VENUE IN THE CENTRE OF BATH

"one of the best places to catch a glimpse of bands before they ascend to dizzy heights."
NME.com

NEWS / REVIEWS / TICKETS / LISTINGS / MEMBERSHIP / FORUM
WWW.MOLES.CO.UK
14 GEORGE STREET, BATH, BA1 2EN / 01225 404445

www.itchybath.co.uk

47

Dance

Delfter Krug
Saw Close
(01225) 443 352

Not only is it a damn fine bar in the day, it's easily Bath's best all-round nightclub, with six days of decent nights on offer for a tiny entry fee. From the high-tech laser light show to booking top name international DJs (Mylo, Andy C and Goldie to name a few) who show off their skills on the best sound system in Bath, DK always gets it right. And with the eclectic music policy, from pop to d 'n' b via indie, there's a night for pretty much everyone here. Unless you thought this venue was entirely something else and turned up expecting topless Germans dancing to tech-trance.
🄯 *Mon–Thu, 12pm–2am; Fri–Sat, 12pm–3am*
🄰 *Prices vary*

Moles
14 George Street
(01225) 404 445

Moles is absolutely the best place for live music and dancing in the city. It's where you'll get the opportunity to see one of those up-and-coming bands that tear the place apart. Musically. They've also showcased some of the big-hitters as well – Oasis tried out some new material on audiences here back in the day. And if that wasn't enough, their knock-out club nights continue to serve the public with fun, frolics and mayhem every night of the week. There's no question, this naughty little underground animal is of the 24hr party variety.
🄯 *Times vary*
🄰 *£3–£7*

Second Bridge

10 Manvers Street

(01225) 464 449

By keeping it over 21s at the weekend, they might be alienating half the population of Bath, but it saves us all from the young ones being sick under our feet, stumbling about, and generally turning every room into a potential case study for *Booze Britain*. What you'll get once you're a tiny bit older is a club that has class cutting through the whole venue, but the music's a little standard. If you're only after the better tunes, it's probably best to hold out for the weeknights when the 18–21s get let back in to run riot. Although that kind of defeats the point we were just trying to make. Oh well.

© *Times and prices vary*

Weir Lounge

Spring Gardens Road

(01225) 447 187

Formerly QTs, the interior may have changed dramatically but the music hasn't, which we're rather thankful for. They have the danciest, most beat-smashing, synth-hitting playlist in town, with nights ranging from garage and r 'n' b, proper hard house and trance, to a mean little drum and bass night, and all blasting out on a sound system as sweet as an angel. It might not be some people's idea of fun, but you'll find us here, dancing in googly-eyed, wet, sweaty crowds. We'll be the ones cutting some awesome shapes in the corner, thanking God that we don't have to endure yet another night of nasty cheese.

© *Times and prices vary*

Gay

Gay

Drag Kings: A Very British Affair

MEN WHO DRESS AS WOMEN ARE OLD HAT. ITCHY'S MUCH MORE OF A FAN OF THE NATION'S NEWEST GAY CRAZE – WOMEN DRESSING AS MEN. MOVE OVER DRAG QUEENS: HERE COME DRAG KINGS

Following its brief moment in the spotlight during Victorian music hall performances, drag king shows – where women dress as men – may have pretty much vanished, but they're just about to make a comeback.

Some king performers take on realistic male personas on the stage by strapping down the chest area, 'packing' (typically created by sock-filled condoms), and adding realistic facial hair. Performances are usually mimed comic songs, performed as a 'troupe' of band members. However, solo performers, who take the act into wilder and more feisty territory, are becoming increasingly common.

Worldwide, 'kinging' has moved on from the days of old, but backward Britannia is still dragging her high heels. Drag queens have long been accepted in the gay scene, and more recently in mainstream entertainment, but sadly drag kings are yet to gain the same widespread popularity.

Illustration by Si Clarke

There is some hope though. The annual Transfabulous Festival is a big showcase for drag kings, and the Wotever World group hosts a variety of different drag king-packed nights. If this risqué revolution does take hold, we reckon there's no reason drag kings shouldn't have as much stage-space as their long-successful queen counterparts. Perhaps the art of female cross-dressing is about to come home...

Gay

PUBS

The Bath Tap

19–20 St James Parade

(01225) 404 344

Although most of the gay community in Bath are flocking to Mandalyns for their nights out, they're still missing out by not giving this place a try. The Bath Tap is closer to the train station for a start, which is convenient for a slightly more alternative pub crawl. Failing that, its situation means that if you're having a really dull time, you're only a hop, skip and a jump away from making a quick getaway by train. It's rarely busy but the atmosphere is great. They even sell poppers behind the bar.

⏰ *Mon–Wed, 12pm–11pm; Thu–Sat, 12pm–2am; Sun, 12pm–10.30pm*

OTHER

The Suite

www.thesuitebath.com

(01225) 465 725

If you like things super-sized, check out The Suite – Bath's only all-male gay sauna. Two minutes from Bath Spa station, it's got everything you need to get you going, offering up larger-than-life facilities, including a 20ft swimming pool, a legendary steam room, sauna, privacy rooms and a new and fully licensed TV/play lounge, ideal for a drink and an X-rated DVD or two. There's even a new 'dark room' so you can develop snaps of your family rambling break in the Peak District. Climb every mounting.

⏰ *Mon–Thu, 11am–11pm; Fri, 11am–Sun, 11pm (24 hours)*

CLUBS

Mandalyns

13 Fountain Buildings, Landsdown Road

(01225) 425 403

This place is gayer than a *Will and Grace* TV marathon, watched through a pink-tinted lens with a rainbow flag border. But screaming as this place is, it's screaming in a very good way. There's plenty to do here; talk to a transvestite, become a transvestite, indulge in a Slippery Dick or a Rampant Rabbit for £4, sing a Cher song or two to an adoring crowd, and that's just for starters; they have handy chalk boards in the loos if you want to leave a cheeky message for someone.

⏰ *Mon–Wed, 4pm–1am; Thu–Fri, 4pm–2am; Sat, 3pm–2am; Sun, 3pm–1am*

Shop

Shop

Welcome to Shop

Help fuel Bath's economy by emptying your purse in one of its many shops. If it's a record that you're after, **Drop Records (27 Broad Street, 01225 444 577)** will serve you up a cool selection of leftfield electronica, dubstep and breaks. For the random and the tatty, **Walcot Flea Market (Walcot Street)** will satisfy your consumerist impulses for less than a fiver. Bath's most bizarre shop has got to be **Vintage to Vogue (28 Milsom Street, 01225 337 323)** where Victorian lace nighties nestle against trilby hats. But boys and girls with retro tastes should head to **Yellow Shop (74 Walcot Street, 01225 404 001)** which does the hard work of charity shopping for you.

Top five bits of tourist tat to buy in Bath

Jane Austen mug – Reflect on why Austen hated Bath as you drink your tea.

Bath bun – This one should be obvious...

Dyson vacuum cleaner – The idea for this dual-cyclone, bag-less wonder was conceived in Bath.

Flagon of cider – The West Country's favourite tipple

Thermae Spa slippers – As comfy at home as they are here...

Top five shops to bag a bargain in

Oxfam Books – More than Danielle Steele on offer here.

Vintage to Vogue – Not only your mum's cast-offs, but your great-grandmother's too.

Walcot Flea Market – Things you never knew you needed.

Yellow Shop – Well-selected vintage garb.

Jack and Dannys – Overflowing with bargains. A good place to kill time finding them.

DEPARTMENT STORES

Jolly's

7–13 Milsom Street

(01225) 426 811

Don't come here if you plan to leave in a hurry. This store's labyrinthine layout encompasses multiple floors overflowing with myriad clothing ranges, cosmetics and accessories, but nary a signpost for the exit. After a couple of hours wandering through racks of designer clobber, we were considering trying to subsist off nutrients from the hems of dresses (well, you haven't tasted the food in their café...). Thank God for that compass we found in a Christmas cracker, that's all we can say.

🕒 *Mon–Sat, 9am–6pm; Tue, 9.30am–6pm; Thu, 9am–7pm; Sun, 11am–5pm*

MARKETS

Bath Food Market

Green Park Station

Gordon Ramsay, Jeremy Clarkson, Jonathan Ross: Itchy likes a bit of arrogance. Which is why we love this place. Bath Food Market's cocksure approach to business saw it setting up shop next to the city's busiest supermarket, and what's more, they got away with it. Expect sausages and vegetables of the highest quality, various animals you'll never find in a supermarket, a fish stall, breadmakers, cheese stands and preserves aplenty. Compared to this, Sainsbury's 'Taste the Difference' range should be renamed, 'Taste the shit in this packet'.

🕒 *Sat, 8.30am–1.30pm*

SHOPPING AREAS

Shires Yard

Milsom Street

(01225) 789 040

For the majority of us, the Yard is used as a shelter from the elements on our way around some far less expensive shopping destinations. For a select few (as in people with masses of coin), you can buy all sorts of expensive trinkets, gadgets and possessions. Personally, we like to spread a hundred pounds around a few purchases, but if you have the money, why not use it? Oh, it's also a nice shortcut to get from Milsom Street to Bond Street without having to climb up the hill.

🕒 *Mon–Sat, 9.30am–5.30pm; Sun, 11am–4pm*

Walcot Flea Market

Walcot Street

(01225) 317 154

A great place to go and browse impractical brass tools and bead jewellery, antiques and 50s radios. There's a little record stall with everything from dance to rockabilly sitting next to a stall that sells boho bric-a-brac and saws. Among the clothes stalls there are 50s heels and 70s coats, and a few throws and furs. Take a deep breath, dive in and hope for the best. We're not joking about the deep breath mind; the stench in here can be worse than your granny's clothes cupboard. Think of it as something between a car boot and a tip: the stuff here isn't junk, but you're unlikely to find the Micro Machines City Itchy always wanted.

🕒 *Sat, 8am–4pm*

Shop

FOOD

Minerva Chocolate
14 Cheap Street
(01225) 464 999

You'd think Itchy would be put off entering any shop with a framed picture of the owner cupping a pair of chocolate boobies, but we're adventurers of the most determined kind. Fortunately, this isn't a novelty sweet shop. This is serious business and there are treats to satisfy the deepest of addictions. It's not cheap, but you'd be foolish to ignore the hot chocolate, as rich as liquid gold. It's not, of course, otherwise it wouldn't do such beautiful things to you internally.

◉ *Mon–Sat, 10.30am–6pm;*
Sun, 11.30am–5pm

The Sweet Shop
8 North Parade Passage
(01225) 477 000

When you get a little bit older, it's hard to recall just how much pleasure you can get from a simple paper bag chock full of sugary sweets. It pains us to think of those days when we would scrape together pocket money and spend so sparingly, because now we have real jobs, we can afford whole jars of the stuff, and make our pockets bulge with everything from gobstoppers to jelly delicacies, pear drops to cola bottles, sherbet lemons to milk teeth, fried eggs to those weird shrimp sweets... oh we forgot something, sorry... <insert Willy Wonka reference and a joke about Oompa Loompas here>.

◉ *Mon–Sat, 10am–5.30pm; Sun, 11am–4pm*

The Sausage Shop
7 Green Street
(01225) 318 300

If you don't know your arse from your elbow when it comes to the hallowed banger, or are still eating those cheapies containing said arseholes and elbows, then we would recommend a trip down here. With over 30 different pork tubes, it's a tough choice, but when they're all traditional and devoid of all the shitty stuff like crushed hooves and retinas, you can't really go far wrong. We would recommend the merguez, but why listen to us when Delia Smith herself has recommended the place. And she's never got anything wrong in her life. Except making a total arse of herself by supporting Norwich City.

◉ *Mon–Sat, 9am–5.30pm*

SHOES

Office
3 Burton Street
(01225) 466 055

All Stars fans will be in heaven here. Any girls as well. For boys who don't like baseball shoes, it's a little bit rubbish to be honest, but if you wear your buffs right down to the wire as we do, it's heading up the best of a bad bunch. Which is kind of tragic really, because their kicks aren't that good. Girls get treated nice, with all the latest shoes and all the styles, so girls, get in and get them; boys, just mope on endlessly about the fact that you have no cool boots. And seeing as girls also get multiple orgasms, feel free to moan about that as well.

◉ *Mon–Sat, 9am–6pm; Sun, 11am–5pm*

BOOKS

Guildhall Market Book Shop

Guildhall Market, High Street

(01225) 477 944

Our favourite place to buy books since we picked up our first cowboys and Indians novel for 40p. When we read about Breed; half-white, half-apache, slaughtering those who had left him for dead, we knew there was no turning back. There are things here you will never find in standard bookshops, and for some reason, they sell all the cooler older pulp novels for pennies. It's a diggers paradise, and it makes you feel like you're getting something no one else can find. Breed would end this with a really sharp closing comment. Um...

Ⓒ *Mon–Sat, 8am–5.30pm*

Waterstone's

4 Milsom Street

(01225) 448 515

What a relaxing name for a bookshop. Sounds like it should be featured in *Around The World in 80 Gardens*, but with books. And cards and wrapping paper thrown in for good measure. Ah, the gift of knowledge.

Ⓒ *Mon–Sat, 9am–7pm; Sun, 11am–5pm*

WH Smith

6–7 Union Street

(01225) 460 522

The WH stands for, 'We Have (everything)'. Okay, so we didn't think that one through, but they do sell all sorts here. Perfect for that back-to-school nostalgia vibe.

Ⓒ *Mon–Fri, 9am–5.30pm; Sat, 9am–6pm; Sun, 11am–5pm*

Mr B's Emporium of Reading Delights

14–15 John Street

(01225) 331 155

Mr B's makes it easy to buy books. In fact, we challenge you to find one that's any easier. Any place that offers you a comfy chair and a cuppa and lets you sit down to preview your purchases is always going to make us want to spend, spend, spend. There's also a toilet if you've been there for a while and had a bit too much of your favourite diuretic. It shouldn't be long until they start offering piggybacks around the shop, launch a free soup kitchen, and then just give the books away to people with nice faces.

Ⓒ *Mon–Wed & Fri–Sat, 9.30am–6.30pm; Thu, 9.30am–8.30pm*

Shop

Oxfam Books

4–5 Lower Borough Walls

(01225) 469 776

Back in the day, when Itchy wanted to find a cheap read, we'd exploit charities for bargain treats. This meant trawling through mountains of Catherine Cookson almost obsessively until we gave up and grabbed anything, just as long as we could escape with our sanity. Luckily, those clever people at Oxfam have stolen all the best books no one wants anymore and set them out alphabetically by genre. Now shopping for secondhand books might even be a pleasurable experience. You won't need to go anywhere else for your books. Unless you want something that was first published in the last 20 years.

⏺ *Mon–Sat, 10am–5pm*

WOMEN'S CLOTHING

Mee

9a Bartlett Street

(01225) 442 250

Honestly, if we tell you about this place, we're going to have to warn you that if you have no self-restraint, then stop reading. Well, unless you're a guy. What does any woman want in a shop? Well, whatever it is, it's all here, from the latest NY fashions to handmade dresses, the toppest heel designers and nap sack makers to a vast array of knick-knacks. As if that wasn't enough, they might try and ply you with booze to loosen those purse strings. They really know every trick in the book...

⏺ *Mon–Sat, 10am–5.30pm; Sun, 11.30am–4.30pm*

MEN'S CLOTHING

Cecil Gee

8–10 Old Bond Street

(01225) 483 443

Right – here's a city with two universities, so that means double your average student population. In this city, there's all kinds of clothes shops which have your standard, dull, bland kinds of clothes – and then there's a handful of places like this, which break a fair few hearts on a daily basis. Waving their designer labels in students' faces, they try and tempt them with their intricately cut shirts, suits, leather bound boots... oh my, it makes us sick. It is all rather nice though, so perhaps that overdraft can stretch a little further.

⏺ *Mon–Sat, 9am–6pm; Sun, 11am–5pm*

Uttam London

12–13 The Corridor

(01225) 442 227

There are some big shoes to fill here, since the previously housed goth-boutique broke a thousand awkward teen hearts and moved to Bristol. So, out with black and white stripes, black lace, black, black, black, black, and in with a few little black dresses and a lot of style, and, refreshingly, a bit of colour that isn't blood red. With some delightful dresses, tops and all kinds of clothy treats, it might have given some troubled teens something else to mew on about, but it's made a lot of girls a lot happier, which really can't be a bad thing now, can it?

⏺ *Mon–Fri, 10am–6pm; Sat, 8.30am–6.30pm; Sun, 9.30am–6.30pm*

UNISEX CLOTHING

Gaff

29 Upper Borough Walls
(01225) 448 585

Perhaps it's about time you threw out those scuffed All Stars, forgot about the jeans that are coming apart at the seams, the T-shirt with the cracked logo and the beanie that's unravelling atop your head. It's going to cost you a fair bit of honk to get kitted out fully, but if this is what you intend to do, might we recommend Gaff? A few classy pieces, a few labels, and all deliciously understocked, so even if all us scruffy young people start dressing a bit nicer, at least we won't all be wearing the same thing.

Ⓒ *Mon–Sat, 10am–5.30pm;*
Sun, 12pm–4.30pm

MB's

The Podium, Northgate Street
(01225) 427 514

Nothing like wearing a wacky T-shirt is there? The way we see it if there's someone with a really funny slogan on their T-shirt, then they're probably great. We just have such a lot of respect for people who don't care at all about fashion in any way and think that wearing something which is supposed to be funny (but is written by someone else) is definitely, really, massively cool. Whether it says something about tits or liking them loads, or something crazy like 'I'm well lazy' or 'I like doing wanks' in a witty way, they probably got it from here. Wicked shop.

Ⓒ *Mon–Sat, 9.30am–6pm;*
Sun, 11am–5pm

Westworld
36 Westgate Street
(01225) 447 006

Outfitters of the urban variety, which basically means T-shirts with heavy logos from companies you don't want to be seen wearing unless you're a student or a 30 year-old with a belly. If that's your kind of thing and floats your fashion boat, then this is some kind of paradise, and there are plenty of label lovers jostling for space around the tiny shop floor. It's more full-blown fighting really, considering there's only enough space for about two people (who aren't swinging cats). Still, they manage to fit it into this lack of space, like it was some kind of TARDIS sponsored by Hooch and Bench.
🕐 *Mon–Sat, 9am–5.30pm; Sun, 11am–5pm*

Yellow Shop
74 Walcot Street
(01225) 404 001

This is an essential place for those too lazy (or rich) to do their own charity shop hunting, bringing together a fine collection of vintage threads and accessories for those not happy with our throwaway culture. There's a separate floor for coats, and the upstairs is wall-to-wall shirts, skirts, trousers and jumpers. It's a heaven for students (and those who are still student-at-heart). The downside is you'll part with a lot more moolah than you would at the bona fide charity shops. The stuff's a fair bit more than a quid an item, but who can put a price on clothes your mum and dad will remember wearing?
🕐 *Mon–Sat, 10.30am–5.30pm*

SECONDHAND

Jack and Danny's
Walcot Street
(01225) 312 345

Itchy likes to see a shop that uses its space creatively. We're so tired of shops that put things neatly on racks or fold garments up so they don't crease and then lay them out so that everyone can see them clearly. Where's the sense of achievement in shopping like that? At Jack and Danny's they cram as much clothing as possible into every possible nook and cranny. This means more special finds per square foot than anywhere else in Bath. With mountains of retro garb, there's something for everyone's dressing-up box here.
🕐 *Mon–Sun, 10.30am–5.30pm*

Vintage to Vogue
28 Milsom Street
(01225) 337 323

Now this is what we mean by vintage clothing. Forget the definition of 'retro' being 60s to 80s, unless of course you're talking about the 19th century. With racks and racks of beautiful garments stretching back to the Victorian era, this is the place to get your retrospective. Among the tails and top hats there's the chance of a real find here, as we discovered in the form of a 50s teddy boy jacket, which we will cherish forever and ever, and may perhaps one day actually work up the courage to wear out. We recommend you come here and become as potentially cool as we could be.
🕐 *Tue–Sat, 10.30am–5pm*

Shop

OTHER

Bijoux Beads
2 Abbey Street
(01225) 482 024

You know when you just need a shopping bag full to the brim with beads and assorted tat? Well, this is the place to go for it. Essentially, if you ever wanted a bead of any size, substance, colour or sexual orientation, they probably have it here. And they have other stuff too, like more things that can be put on jewellery and clothes. And if you've never been confident threading a bead onto a piece of string, then the staff are full of useful advice. More than that, they even hold classes dedicated to expanding your bead creativity.
Mon–Sat, 10am–5pm; Sun, 11am–4.30pm

Hansel und Gretel
9 Margarets Buildings
(01225) 464 677

There's something incredibly endearing about this place. Bizarre as it seems, the feel of a nice object made out of wood does something to our insides (see how we avoided a joke about getting wood there?), or maybe it's that we always have to go and eat in the strudel bar downstairs, and fill ourselves up on fluffy alpine delicacies. From cuckoo clocks and wooden toys to northern Euro knick-knacks, it's all housed inside this pretty little shop. You'll need to go and see it with your own eyeballs to appreciate fully, mind. Just don't start nibbling on the shop front though. They hate that.
Mon–Sat, 10am–5.30pm; Sun, 11am–3pm

Frederick Tranters
5 Church Street
(01225) 466 197

Get off the Lambert & Butler and start treating your pock-addled lungs to some real tobacco. Surely if you're going to murder yourself, then it should be done in an overtly pompous way, with handmade cigarettes, blended tobaccos, pipe tobaccos, flavoured tobaccos and all manner of incarnations of the evil weed. They also sell paraphernalia, such as pipes, lighters and hip flasks. They really have thought of everything. Now you can smash your liver up wherever you go. One day we hope we can afford one of their insanely expensive cigars, but we think that it's probably just a pipe dream. Sorry.
Mon–Sat, 9am–5pm

Lush
12 Union Street
(01225) 428 271

Humanely tested and intensely scented – a shop that aims for bath time perfection. Warning – you will probably want to eat everything here, but that would be bad for you. They sell the type of smellies and soaps that you probably wouldn't want to waste when it comes to washing your hands after a big number two, rather the type you'd keep for those special occasions, like a romantic bath with a loved one that seems like a good idea at the time, until you get wedged up against the taps and have to use up all your expensive soaps to assist your unsticking. What a waste.
Mon–Fri, 9.30am–5.30pm; Sat, 9am–6pm; Sun, 11am–5pm

Octopus

5 Old Bond Street

(01225) 462 372

There's something sinister going on here. Every time we go in here we want to buy another lighter or clock, or some strange, coloured object that we will probably just lose or forget about. It's as if the shock of getting our retinas punched by whacked out colours and shapes is leaving us too weak to resist another expensive toaster or a kooky umbrella. Don't let us put you off though. If you like garish designs and offensive colours slapped on everything you own then you won't get a better shop. For those people who think crazy appliances spell class.

🕐 *Mon–Fri, 9am–6pm; Sat, 9am–7pm;*
Sun, 10.30am–5pm

Tumi

8–9 New Bond Street Place

(01225) 464 736

A pretty place, full of exotic finery from all over South America. It's hard not to get sucked into the rhythm of the rhumba busting out the jukebox. You may suddenly find yourself desiring a random bit of pottery, or else feeling inexplicably drawn to a musical instrument that you have no intention of ever learning how to play, but will leave lying around your flat for people to ask you about anyway. Add to these other unusual treasures such as jewellery, furniture, and the coolest hats we have ever clapped eyes on among all manner of handmade artefacts, and you'll be dying to find a carnival to pop off to.

🕐 *Mon–Sat, 9.30am–6pm; Sun, 12pm–6pm*

Space NK

10 New Bond Street

(01225) 482 804

Some people would say that beauty comes from within, but we always imagine those people to have horrible faces. For the rest of us shallow and insecure folk, we need to get out there and use everything we can to trick people into thinking we're better looking than we actually are. There's all kinds of slop here to intensify or hide the various angles and protrusions of your face, including those eight rather unsightly chins you've been trying to hide. From the very expensive to the not-quite-as-expensive, all the products here are incredibly effective. No one said being beautiful was going to be cheap.

🕐 *Mon–Sat, 9.30am–6pm; Sun, 11am–5pm*

Out & About

Out & About

Welcome to Out & About

Set in the rolling hills of the West, it makes sense to take advantage of Bath's beautiful views from on high; give **Bath Balloons (01225 466 888)** a call to arrange a hot air balloon ride. Laugh until you cry at the **Comedy Cavern (Porter Cellar Bar, George Street, 01225 424 104)**. Don't be put-off by the fact that 'Jimmy Carr started out here', there's a lot more on offer. **The Ghost Walk (01225 350 512)** has got to be Bath's best attraction – a truly hair-raising way to improve your pub quiz knowledge. Or, if you're a vulture for a bit of culture, visit **The Theatre Royal (Sawclose, 01225 448 844)** for both timeless classics and some newer pieces.

Top five summer activities

Pultney Bridge – The bridge looks great, but the shops on it are crap. Visit in good weather so you won't have to go into any of them.

Ghost Walk – The hairs on your neck will stand up from fear.

Royal Victoria Gardens – Skate park, botanical garden, crazy golf, real golf and a 360-degree seesaw.

Longleat – Watch in awe as a gaggle of monkeys dent the bonnet of your car.

Bath Balloons – The ultimate way to view this beautiful city.

Top five winter activities

Thermae Bath Spa – Sit in the outdoor thermal spa while it snows – pure decadence.

Beaux Arts – Great contemporary art that you'll want above your mantelpiece.

Assembly Rooms and Costume Museum – Take window-shopping to a whole new level.

Rondo Theatre – A daring antidote to the somewhat predictable Theatre Royal.

Moles – The best place for live music in the city. Say no more.

Itchy's Dictionary
of *Dahling!*

EVER FELT THAT THE CULTURE-SAVVY SEEM TO DWELL ON A HIGHER INTELLECTUAL PLANE THAN THE REST OF US? WELL NEVER FEAR – BEHIND THEIR LUVVIE LINGO, REFINED-SOUNDING FOLK HAVE THE SAME THOUGHTS, HOPES AND FEARS AS US CRUDE PROLETARIANS. HAVE A PEEP AT ITCHY'S THESP THESAURUS TO FIND OUT WHAT THEY'RE REALLY ON ABOUT.

ON THEATRE

'I found the final act deeply moving.' *The end was just like* Last of the Mohicans.

'His sense of comic timing left something to be desired.' – *I've had funnier episodes of food poisoning.*

'I felt the costumes were rather avant-garde.' – *I could almost see Juliet's nipples in that corset.*

ON MUSIC

'I don't much care for their notion of ensemble.' – *I'm going to piss in a bottle and throw it at the drummer.*

'I've always had a sense of vocation about the arts.' – *Why don't we start a band? I've got an old cowbell I stole from school and you could play the harmonica.*

ON DANCING

'Oh my, I'm all left feet this evening!' *We both know that I was dry-humping your leg just then, but let's never speak of it again, eh?*

'Nothing like a foxtrot to aid one's constitution.' – *I'm shagged. Where's the bar?*

ON WINE

'This wine's really got legs.' – *And I won't when I've had enough of it.*

'A young and bold number, with zesty notes of rosemary and field mushroom.' – *This one was the second cheapest on the menu.*

ON ART GALLERIES

'I find the figurative liberties of proto-classical sculpture highly diverting.' – *Hee hee, look at the massive wanger on that statue. I wonder if they sell replicas in the shop.*

Illustration by Si Clarke

Out & About

CINEMAS

The Little Theatre
St Michaels Place
(01225) 330 817

When the manager greets you on entry it means he's got something to be proud of. It's beautiful inside and the atmosphere is one of happy anticipation. They'll put on the odd mainstream film, but it's mainly independent and international cinema. Become a member and you'll get free tickets, special offers and £2 off entry. They let members pick films to screen and they even serve ethical sweets. A good place to come and impress that special someone who thinks you're an uncultured booze hound.

☻ *Mon–Sun, 10.30am–9.30pm*
🎫 *£6.70; concs, £5.50*

COMEDY

Comedy Cavern
Porter Cellar Bar, George Street
(01225) 424 104

'Jimmy Carr started out here' is the boast of this place. Thankfully, no one we've ever seen here is quite as shit as him. It's a claim that's really not doing them any favours, surely, as anyone who's a massive Jimmy Carr fan will be at home watching him deadpan his way through a Channel 4 compilation list. Comedy nights are a mixed bag, and some nights will be funnier than others, but why wouldn't you come here all the time when you're only passing over a few quid to have people make you laugh?

☻ *Sun, 7.30pm–late*
🎫 *£7; concs, £6*

The Odeon
James Street West
(0871) 224 4007

Ugly kids will sell you overpriced tickets to mainstream films. They'll sting you on food and drink, but if you don't buy any, your date will think you're cheap and miserable. At least the seats are comfortable, but maybe you'll get one just under the air conditioning, or the heating, which will freeze or burn you respectively. And you'll more than likely want to go bananas at some bastard who doesn't understand the social etiquette of watching films quietly. Snobbish, perhaps, but this place is a real pain in our arses, and they have us over a barrel, because watching films is our standard third date.

☻ *Times and dates vary*

LIVE MUSIC

Moles Club

14 George Street

(01225) 404 445

Moles is absolutely the best place for live music and dancing in the city. It's where you'll get the opportunity to see one of those up-and-coming bands that tear the place apart. Musically, They've also showcased some of the big-hitters as well – Oasis tried out some new material on audiences here back in the day. And if that wasn't enough, their knock-out club nights continue to serve the public with fun, frolics and mayhem every night of the week.

☻ *Times vary*

☻ £3–£7

THEATRE

Rondo Theatre

St. Saviours Road, Larkhall

(01225) 444 003

With a theatre this small, it can go two ways. Having performers practically acting on your lap can potentially engage you in just about anything. On the other hand, if it's quite terrible, then there's not a chance of you escaping unnoticed. And if you just want to try and sleep through the whole damn thing, you can't. Luckily, the majority of what goes on here isn't too shoddy: good productions which are well-acted. We recommend booking early. Unless you're a true thesp and you want to leave it right 'til the last minute.

☻ £6–£8

The Pavillion

North Parade Road

(01225) 330 304

Although it sometimes feels like watching the end of your garden for the fairies to appear, every so often something comes along here that might just be worth the wait. Among regular keep fit, roller skating, Elvis tributes and line dancing nights, a band or two will play here, maybe even the odd DJ worth their salt. We're not promising anything, mind, but we did see Mr Scruff here once and that was pretty nice. We wake up with our fingers crossed every morning, hoping someone of some calibre will once again return to our fair Pav and make us proud of it once more, the way we should be.

☻ *Times and prices vary*

Theatre Royal

Sawclose

(01225) 488 844

The Theatre Royal has had plenty of time to establish itself, what with it being one of the oldest venues in the country and everything. They've taken that time to develop a brochure full of productions for every person ever in existence, from the complete dunce to the painfully high brow, as well as everyone in between. There's everything from Shakespeare to sing-along *Sound of Music* here. Personally, we're not sophisticated enough for any Harold Pinter or anything, we much prefer the pantomime – which is our favourite. 'Oh no it isn't!' Yeah ok, we lied.

☻ *Box office, Mon–Sat, 10am–8pm;*
Sun, 12pm–8pm

Out & About

MUSEUMS

Museum of Costume
Bennett Street
(01225) 477 789

This place is a hotbed of fashion, whether you decide to direct your attention to the glass cabinets or the patrons. You can either opt to see 500 years of high style, or else the decade-late mistakes of the European tourists, complete with their knee-high socks and brown sandals. Oh, when will they learn? Audio guides accompany your visit, and it's a 2-4-1 as well with the Assembly Rooms, which gives you an idea of where very rich people used to go for rave ups and discos back in the day. Value.

🕓 *Mon–Sun, 11am–5pm*
💷 *Adults, £6.50*

Jane Austen Museum
40 Gay Street, Queens Square
(01225) 443 000

'It will be two years tomorrow since we left Bath for Clifton, with what happy feelings of escape.' So wrote Jane Austen, who hated Bath so much it made her feel nauseous. And the only people in her books who like Bath are idiots. Good job for whoever decided to set up a museum dedicated to all things Jane Austen in the one place she was least happy. We would say don't go here unless you're a tourist, because it's tacky and tasteless, and especially not if you're a big fan, because it's as bad as spitting (or worse) on her grave.

🕓 *Mon–Fri & Sun, 11am–4.30pm;*
Sat, 9.45am–5.30pm
💷 *£6.50; concs, £4.95*

Bath at Work
Camden Works, Julian Road
(01225) 318 348

History. Sometimes just a massively aimless pit of nonsensical information. Here, we get the chance to see 2,000 years of how people earned wedge, alongside a recreated Victorian engineering working environment. Mildly fascinating, mainly due to the fact there's a full size model of a stone mine, if just for the fact that its creation could have just been done with drawings or papier-maché or something. Still, if you like watching old things working, and frankly, who doesn't, then you won't find a better place for it in the city.

🕓 *1st Apr–31st Oct, Mon–Sun, 10.30am–4pm; 1st Nov–31st March, weekends only*
💷 *£4; concs, £3*

PARKS

Royal Victoria Park
Below Royal Crescent

Possibly the best day location in Bath is the parks. There's always somewhere for even the most skint to congregate and have some fun. Take the opportunity to demonstrate your sporting prowess to your friends and try a spot of football, rounders or Frisbee. You might even make a start on that last bit of flab you keep promising yourself you're about to lose for that party. Victoria Park is the very best, with acres and acres of grassy paradise to while away a sunny afternoon. There's botanical gardens, a skate park, crazy golf, real golf and possibly the best playground ride ever created.

GALLERIES

Beaux Arts

12–13 York Street
(01225) 464 850

It's a bit intimidating here, inasmuch as everything here is on sale and we'll never be able to afford it. Still, we wish we could because there are a fair few top quality artists on display here. You'll see everything, from beautiful oil paintings to metal sculpture and ceramics, from the berserk to the sublime. Luckily, it's free to get in, so you could dress up in your most expensive outfit and pretend you might be able to buy one at some point in the future. Some would call that delusional, but we'll say optimistic.

◉ *Mon–Sat, 10am–5pm*
🎫 *Free*

Victoria Art Gallery

Bridge Street
(01225) 477 772

Named after Queen Victoria, around since 1897 (the gallery that is, not Queen Victoria), the Victoria Art Gallery is the receiver of around 92,000 visitors annually. Why so many? Well, as far as we can work out, it's so they can gawp at a collection of 150 china dogs. We can't think what else they're here for, because frankly the china dogs are mad as a hat and well worth a look. Oh, you could also come for regularly updated exhibitions, or paintings, sculpture and so on from (mainly local) artists such as Turner.

◉ *Tue–Fri, 10am–5.30pm; Sat, 10am–5pm; Sun, 2pm–5pm*
🎫 *Free*

SPORT

Bath City Football Club

Twerton Park
(01225) 313 247

We have a real taste for low-grade sports, perfectly poised between depressing and the best thing ever, and we can't explain why really. Perhaps it's the fact that mostly the players play like they have rickets and they're kicking a ball around that's actually a pig's bladder filled with iron shot, so their little soft limbs just disintegrate and fold over on themselves and so on. Perhaps it's just that they really try to play, and they're not playing for money, but for love, or expression, or laughs or something, and that fills our hearts with rapture.
🎫 *£6–£11*

Out & About

Bath Rugby Club
The Recreation Ground
(01225) 325 200

It's nice to have a sporting team in the city that achieves something (that was aimed at you, Bath City FC). If you're not into rugby already, then now really is the time to start. To put it in perspective, last season Bath came 8th, which puts them on a level with Reading in the football premiership. No, it's good. At one point they were the Man Utd of rugby, winning the premiership countless times. Admittedly that was in the 80s, but past glories are still glories, right? They have internationally capped players... and if that doesn't convince you, then they have six bars at the ground and you can shout as much as you like.
🄑 £15–£34

The Roman Baths
Abbey Churchyard
(01225) 477 785

Seeing as you're here, you might as well visit the only reason the city exists. Today it drags in as many as it ever did, but now it's lorry loads of tourists in garish continental fashions strolling around slack-jawed at the historical beauty of the site. To some it may look like a pile of bricks, but to people with real minds it means real history, and an understanding of a great empire that helped shape the world as it is today, through art, architecture, politics... sorry, yes, those little audio guides have made us incredibly boring. Knowledgeable, but very, very, dull.
🄒 Mon–Sun, 9am–6pm
🄑 £10.25; concs, £8.75

TOURIST ATTRACTIONS

Bizarre Bath
Outside The Huntsman pub, North Parade Passage
(01225) 335 124

Created in reaction to the incredibly functional and less-than-entertaining tours our foreign cousins endure, Bizarre Bath is all about 'having a bloody laugh' with a wacky comedy tour guide. Not funny as in actually funny, but more funny as in the corners of our mouths creased ever so slightly, possibly in an ironic fashion. And you'll feel more guilty laughing at it than you would a regular tour. It is however a nice way to get accustomed to Bath and collect some facts about the city.
🄒 Mon–Sun, 8pm–9.30pm (Mar–Nov)
🄑 £7; concs, £5

The Ghost Walk
Outside The Garricks Head, Barton Street
(01225) 350 512

Have you ever seen a shadowy figure at the end of your bed? Last night's pull leaving hastily? Even if you're not the next Derek Acorah, suspend your disbelief and you will be chilled to the bone. Around the most haunted spots in Bath you'll meet suicidal brides and a sinister man in a black hat. Just like any other night in Bath you might say, but no, it's not a fancy dress night at the union, these are real, honest-to-God (and we hope they were) dead people. Dress warmly and pray they don't stop outside your house.
🄒 1st Apr–31st Oct, Mon–Sat, 8pm–10pm; 1st Nov–31st Mar, Fri only, 8pm–10pm
🄑 £6; concs, £5

EVENTS AND FESTIVALS

Taste of Bath Festival

www.visitbath.co.uk

In the song *Food, Glorious Food*, written by the late, great Lionel Bart, we feel he left out an important verse. This verse would have extolled the virtues of becoming a human vulture at a food festival, poaching scraps of samplers with much gusto. This is, without a shadow of a doubt, the best kind of festival known to man, all based around the premise of sampling signature dishes from all the best restaurants in the South West. Sure beats tromping round a muddy field hoping to bump into Kate Moss. We salivate at the prospect of doing it year in, year out.

◐ July

Fringe Festival

Edinburgh's not the only place with a Fringe Festival, y'know. And this one's half the length of Edinburgh so it doesn't outstay its welcome quite like that jaded Mandarin. This is England's oldest Fringe Festival and it's like a jumble sale of art events. Theatre, comedy, dance, music, exhibitions and street performers all sitting under one flag. If you can dream it up, someone dressed in a wacky T-shirt is probably performing it. It's a bit of a cultural smorgasbord, and like the best smorgasbords it can get a bit much at times, but you won't regret it, especially as a lot of it is free. Apparently they just get paid by seeing smiling faces. Bit wanky, but as long as we don't have to pay.

◐ May–June

Film Festival

(01225) 401 149

Bath isn't Cannes and you won't find any stars milling around who you will know anything about. Perhaps a director will do a speech before a film, maybe someone from some iconic film you've vaguely heard of but have never seen will show up. It's all about a massive range of world and independent cinema that the multiplexes wouldn't dare show you. So this is your only chance. Some are good, some not so, but with so many going on, there's going to be something there for you, as long as you aren't one of those terrible kids who watches *Epic Movie* or *Transformers*. Then we would advise you to stay away. You will be too stupid.

◐ November

Out & About

FURTHER AFIELD

Bath Balloons
8 Lambridge, London Road
(01225) 466 888

From up on high you can check out all the sights our delightful valley has to offer. Bath is visually stunning from the ground, but the views from up high will make you choke your heart out they are so beautiful. If views aren't your thing you can always just spit at people, or hijack it and try for the fastest circuit of the world, picking up bizarre travelling companions like Jackie Chan. For the same amount you could visit the Baths ten times. Now which would you rather do? Fly a balloon or go to the Baths ten times?

£99–£145

Bristol
If Bath is mummy's little blue-eyed pretty boy, then Bristol is the older, naughtier brother – far edgier and probably started listening to grime, hitting on speed and looking at mucky pictures on the internet at school. It's only a ten minute ride on the train and it's practically another world compared to our tourist-friendly city streets. The music scene here is bigger and more diverse, as are the pubs, the bars, the restaurants, the people, the atmosphere, the activities... it goes on. We're not saying we don't love our little Bath to bits, but, you know, sometimes it's just nice to hang out with the older kids for an evening. We suggest you make the trip every now and then, just to keep life from getting boring.

Longleat
The Estate Office, Longleat
(01985) 844 400

If you ever fancied yourself as a bit of a Hemingway but never had the money to get out to Africa and do a bit of nature baiting, then Longleat is for you. Longleat is Britain's best safari park, created by the mad bastard that is Lord Bath. It's a typically British version of a safari, from naughty monkeys that rip cars apart to really old lions who look like they wouldn't have the energy to devour you even if you happened to fall over and knock yourself out right next to them. It's no wild and dangerous *Jumanji* affair but it's loads of fun nonetheless.

Tours every hour from 11am–3pm

£16–£22

OTHER

Bath Boating Station

Forester Road

(01225) 312 900

A fine way to get about, is boating. Canoes, skiffs and all manner of nautical vessels are on offer, but if you don't feel confident enough to don a pair of deck shoes and get an anchor tattoo quite yet, there's the guided tours that set off hourly, where you can shirk all the marine responsibilities and sit back. Some of the vessels even have drinks and toilets available, which is a revelation/better than pissing off the side. Whether it's a solo mission or a tour-guided cruise up the Avon, this is the place to set sail.

🕐 *Mon–Sun, 10am–6pm*

💷 *£7 per hour*

Royal Crescent

Royal Crescent

(01225) 823 333

With a Grade 1 listing that puts its importance up there with Buckingham Palace in the National Trust stakes (although the Queen would probably have something to say about that), and countries and countries worth of tourists turning up year round to drive past it, there must be something to the place. Apart from its aesthetic aspects, which are numerous and beauteous, there's a museum dolled up like it would have been in the past, all pretty like. All very interesting for historicals and people of that nature. And failing all else, there's a bath house which focuses on the elements of earth, air, fire and water. Apparently.

Pulteney Bridge

One of only four bridges in the world that supports shops across the whole length. Yes, this truly is South West England's answer to the Ponte Vecchio (kind of). It's a marvel of modern engineering crossed with the intricacy and stylistic flourish of Georgian architecture. Unfortunately, the shops and restaurants on the bridge are generally rubbish. Fancy some tweed? Some miniature books? Model cars? Healing crystals? Avoid the actual shops, and if you just look at it, it is very, very nice. In fact, this is a fine example of one of those places that is so much better when viewed from a distance. When you're actually here, it's pretty crap. But viewed from a little way down the river, it's awesome (and there is no other word for it).

Laters

You Snooze, You Lose

MISSING OUT ON LATE-NIGHT FUN BECAUSE YOUR GROOVY TRAIN IS STUCK IN LAZY TOWN? WANNA BE A MEMBER OF THE WIDE AWAKE CLUB, BUT YOUR DOZY HEAD FEELS HEAVIER THAN MALLETT'S MALLET? YOU NEED ITCHY'S MINI A-TO-ZED OF WAYS TO STAY AWAKE FOR DAYS…

If you don't want to set foot in the Land of Nod for a whole 24 hours, preparation must begin at breakfast time. If, like us, you like to kick your day off with a Weetabix or two, you'll know that dried-up cereal is one of the stickiest, most viciously viscous substances known to man. Smear a little porridge onto your eyelids and press them up towards your brows. Next, hold your head over the toaster to accelerate the drying process. Result: your peepers will be glued open permanently, or until it rains.

Worrying is a great way to stave off the sandman. Want to stay wired throughout a week-long holiday or festival? Go for an STD test just before things kick off. It'll be an agonising seven days before your results come through, during which time you won't sleep a wink.

Threadworms are known to be more active at night. Pick up your own wriggly-ass infestation by babysitting for your neighbourhood's grubbiest kids, then enjoy hours of sleeplessness courtesy of an intensely itchy bum. It's guaranteed you'll still be up at the – ahem – 'crack' of dawn.

Or, watch that kinky home video you discovered in your ma and pa's camcorder collection. Better than any horror film for making sure you'll never sleep again.

Illustration by Si Clarke

LATE-NIGHT SHOPPING

For shopaholics whose habit cannot be satisfied by the regular 9–5 opening times, it's worth noting that Thursday is Bath's official late-opening day, when most of the high-street staples will stay open until 9pm. **Jolly's (7–13 Milsom Street, 01225 462 811)**, Bath's warren-like department store is open until 6pm every evening (and 7pm on Thursdays). If you need a new bedtime read, get yourself along to **Mr B's Emporium Of Reading Delights (14–15 John Street, 01225 331 155)** – it's open until 6.30pm Friday to Wednesday and 8.30pm on Thursdays.

LATE-NIGHT DRINKING

When it's kicking out time but you've had one too many to face going home, we suggest you head to **The Common Room (2 Saville Row, 01225 425 550)**. With a chilled atmosphere and good music to match, you'll be pleased that this place is open 'til 2am at weekends. **Po Na Na (8–9 North Parade, 01225 424 952)** is a crowd pleaser. A little dance floor for the energetic, and the sitters will find Moroccan cushions to sink into as well. Looking for something more low-key? You can enjoy your premium Bath Ale until 1am at the **Salamander (3 John Street, 01225 428 889)**.

POST CLUB ACTION

If it's late, but you still feel it's too early for the taxi home, walk off the impending hangover by strolling along the **Royal Crescent** where you'll get the best nighttime views of Bath, possibly enhanced by an alcoholic haze. Reflect on the evening's events over a sobering coffee at **Same, Same But Different (7a Princes Building, 01225 466 856)**, or recline with a mint tea and a plate of delicious and sticky baklava at the brilliant **Arabesque Restaurant (16 Northgate Street, 01225 481 333)**.

FOOD NOW!

If you like your nibbles served with the hottest tunes, **The Adventure Bar and Café (5 Princes Buildings, George Street, 01225 462 038)** will not disappoint, as it's open 'til 12am, Thu–Sat. But if it's the dulcet tones of the Moulin Rouge that you're after, **Café Retro (18 York Street, 01225 339 347)** will give you a croissant and coffee until 11pm, Thu–Sat. For an unusual evening snack, head next door to **The Real Italian Ice Cream Company (17 York Street, 01225 330121)** where you can enjoy a cornet of your choice 'til late. However, if only grease can stop that hangover in its tracks, call **Pizza Hut (1–3 Westgate Building, 01225 448 586)** for late-night deliveries straight to your door.

OTHER LATE-NIGHT INDULGENCES

Want to stay out late without frequenting one of Bath's many pubs? There are a few activities that are best enjoyed without beer. For example? Roller disco nights at **The Pavillion (124 Walcot Street, 01225 486 902)**, where drinking beforehand is far from advisable. Enjoy an off-beat film at **The Little Theatre (1–2 St Michaels Place, 01225 330 817)**. Catch a band at **Moles (14 George Street, 01225 404 405)**. Or else, watch the stars as you soak in the **Thermae Bath Spa's outdoor pool (Hot Bath Street, 01225 331 234)**, which is open 'til 10pm daily.

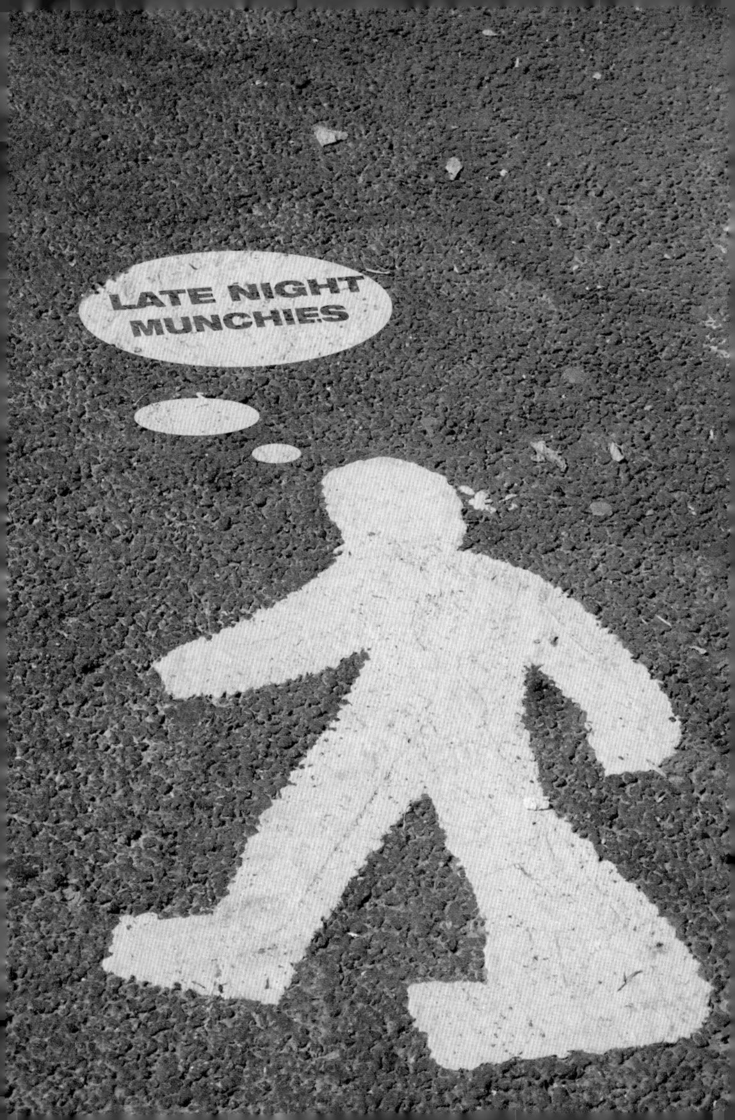
LATE NIGHT
MUNCHIES

Sleep

Sleep

CHEAP

Bath Backpackers Hotel
13 Pierrepont Street
(01225) 466 787
The building's three centuries old, but the business is bang up to date. We like the new shower block and free breakfasts.
From £15.50

St Christophers
Green Street
(01225) 481 444
We like to think that staying above a pub is a really swell idea. While there's always a risk of noisy punters, this one's alright, and there's late opening just in case you need a few nightcaps.
From £18

Bath YMCA
International House, Broad Street Place
(01225) 325 913
You don't need to be Christian, young or even a man to stay here. With good facilities and a central location, secure a room here and you'll be throwing your arms in the air.
From £15

YHA
Bathwick Hill
(08707) 705 688
All the mod cons and a little out of the firing line of the city centre. Considering the fact that for £13 a night we would probably sleep in a small shed or under a large amount of moss, we don't think it's a bad deal at all.
From £13

MID-RANGE

Dorian House

1 Upper Oldfield Park

(01225) 426 336

They aim for 'opulence'. We think 'up their own arse', but have to concede that all in all, it's a fine place for the price bracket.

£ *From £65*

Moonraker Narrowboats

7 Lower East Hayes, London Road

(07973) 876 891

You've got to think outside the box if you want the most out of a bed, and what's further out than a mobile hotel on water? Enjoy the run of the river, the entertainment system and the Jacuzzi. No shit. A Jacuzzi.

£ *From £675 for a short break*

SWANKY

The Royal Crescent Hotel

16 Royal Crescent

(01225) 823 333

The perfect location, all kinds of snootery, numerous awards and a hefty price tag make it not the place for us, dear friends.

£ *From £305*

The Bath Spa Hotel

Sydney Road

(08704) 008 222

If you can afford this place then we don't know why you're reading this. On second thoughts, we suppose you probably don't know how to spend all that lovely money, so read on.

£ *From £171*

Marlborough House

1 Marlborough Lane

(01225) 318 175

Huge Georgian guesthouse just off Victoria Park, every room has an ensuite and four posters. They treat you well, with sherry and cookies on arrival. Like Santa. It's the things like that that make us like places.

£ *From £45*

The Parade Park

8–10 North Parade

(01225) 463 384

Fantastic value for a place right in the middle of town, so it's easy to get to from pretty much anywhere. It's attached to Lambretta's bar as well, so you can stagger home with ease.

£ *From £40*

If You're Starting from Scratch
You'd better get
Itchy

Baltis in Birmingham?,
Cocktails in Cardiff?,
Gigs in Glasgow?

For the best features and
reviews of where to go all
over the UK, log on to:
www.itchycity.co.uk

Useful info

HAIRDRESSERS

Guildhall Barber Shop

Stall 34, Guildhall Market

(01225) 316 065

Lo and behold, these people cut your hair. And if you're lucky, you'll leave looking a lot cooler/less like a yeti than when you went in.

🕒 *Mon–Fri 9am–5pm; Sat, 9am–5.30pm*

Yasmin Meyrick Hairdressing

3 Upper Borough Walls

(01225) 427 666

Set aside any thoughts of that obese, horse-loving misogynist of a man John McCririck, they'll make you look like a beauty here. Or at least they'll try their best.

🕒 *Mon–Wed & Sat, 9am–5pm;*
Thu–Fri, 9am–7pm

Toni and Guy

31 Southgate

(01225) 329 555

We very much doubt that either Toni or Guy have ever been to their Bath branch, but we know people who have and they had very nice haircuts. They ought to be very proud of it.

🕒 *Mon–Fri, 9am–7pm; Sat, 9am–6pm*

INTERNET CAFÉS

DiscoverIT

7a York Street

(01225) 463 030

Green Net

Green Park Station

(01225) 481 015

BODY

Fitness First

5–10 James Street West

(0870) 898 8112

Pump it, pump it. Swimming pool included. We've heard if you give out flyers you might just get a free membership.

🕒 *Mon–Fri, 6.30am–10pm; Sat–Sun, 8am–8pm*

YMCA

Broad Street Place

(01225) 325900

We're sure there's something about getting toned in the Bible. Was Jesus a buff 'ting? All mod-cons and cheap prices make this a good choice.

🕒 *Mon–Fri, 6.30am–10pm;*
Sat–Sun, 8.30am–7pm

TAXIS

V Cars

9 Terrace Walk

(01225) 464 646

If you can't remember this simple number after a few beers, make sure you have these guys on speed dial. Itchy's favourite taxi service works its socks off, running round the clock to pick you up and drop you off in the time it takes to text your mates to say you left your credit card behind the bar. All of their cars have GPS, air conditioning and up to eight seats. Their priority customer booking service allows you to register pick-up points, so their professional, uniformed drivers will know where to fetch you from as soon as you call.

🕒 *24hr service*

PLANES

Bristol International Airport
(0870) 121 2747
Wait, where are you going? Come back...

London Heathrow Airport
(0870) 000 0123
They'll get you just about anywhere.

BUSES

Bath Bus Co Ltd
(01225) 330 4444
Sightseeing tours of Bath, by bus.

First Bus Services
(0845) 606 4446
Much nicer than driving yourself.

TRAINS

First Great Western
(08457) 000 125
Not so great. But definitely Western.

Bath Spa Railway Station
(08457) 484 950
Time to hit that ol' darn railroad.

CAR HIRE

Enterprise Rent-a-Car
(01225) 444 292
Call and ask if they'll rent you a starship.

National Car Rental 3
(01225) 481 898
What happened to one and two?

Useful info

Domino's Pizza

66 Walcot Street

(01225) 421 421

Do we need to say anything here or have they stopped doing those rubbish cartoon bits on *The Simpsons*? If not, then we can only hope that they come tumbling down like a house of cards.

Sun–Thu, 11am–12am; Fri–Sat, 11am–1am

Marmaris

4 Grand Parade,

(01225) 461 964

Reputedly the best kebab there is going, unless you were to actually head off to Marmaris of course. But that seems like a bit too much effort. Head here instead to get your fix of various greasy meaty treats.

Mon–Sun, 11am–11pm

Peking Chinese

1–2 New Street, Kingsmead Square

(01225) 461 750

A Chinese restaurant with the word 'Peking' in the title. It's not every day you see that is it? Ahem. We just found this place all casual like. There we were, peking at the menu... oh yeah, we went there.

Mon–Sun, 12pm–2pm & 6pm–11.15pm

Seafoods

38 Kingsmead Street

(01225) 465 190

Now we like eating cod here at Itchy, but when you eat it, don't you ever feel like it's a bit... natural? Thank God they have people to coat it in batter for you and then give you some fat chips to go with it.

Mon–Sat, 11.30am–10pm

Moghul Indian Takeaway

140 Walcot Street

(01225) 464 956

Situated on Walcot Street, this place has no link to the footballer of the same surname. Our national favourite comes from this, our Bath favourite... or standard, but we feel like that was a better play on words.

Mon–Sun, 5.30pm–12am

Mr D

37 Monmouth Street

(01225) 426 111

We reckon that this place is far better than its almost namesake, and given that it also has a van on Milsom Street, it means that there's no excuse not to go with the D.

Sun–Thu, 11.30am–1am;
Fri–Sat, 11.30am, 3am

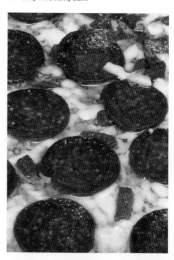

Support

24-hour Locksmith
Bath Lock and Key
Avenue Place, Combe Down
(01225) 835 500

24-hour Electrician
Fox Electrical Contractors
21 Shophouse Road
(01225) 343 530

24-hour Plumber
24:Hour Ultimate Plumbing
(01225) 650 002
(07717) 675 721

A & E Department
St Martins Hospital
(01225) 831 500

Royal United Hospital
(01225) 428 331

Bath NHS Dental Access
Centre
Bluecoat House
(01225) 329 647

Samaritans
(08457) 909 090

Local Police
Bath Police Station
(0845) 456 7000

Family Planning Clinic
Bath Life Care Group
(01225) 832 378

Citizen Advice Bureau
(01225) 463 333

24-hour Pharmacy
Alliance Pharmacy
(01225) 858 753

Student Welfare/Union
Connexions
(01225) 161 501

Rape Helpline
Off The Record
(01225) 312 481

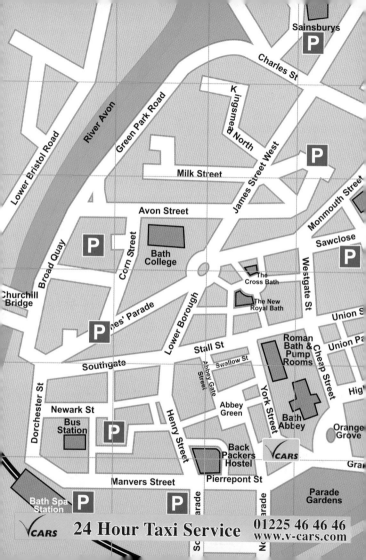

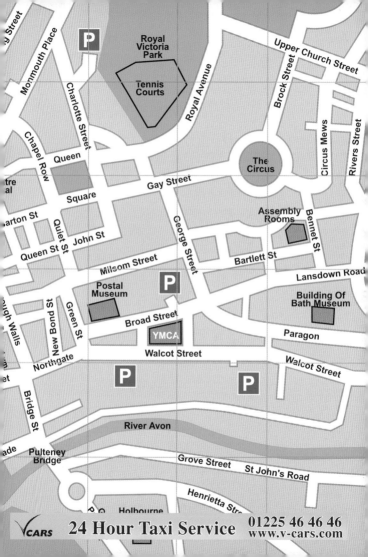

Index